ROSCOE:

MY CARDINAL SIN

A Book for Bird Lovers

By **Chip Kirkpatrick**

PROLOGUE

Cardinals appear when angels are near. Unknown.

A bird in the bush is worth two in the hand. Florida Wildlife Commission

This is a true story. Well, mostly. I have changed a few minor details, mainly to protect the guilty and to avoid costly litigation.

I had no intention of putting this to paper but a number of Roscoe's fans demanded it and I hate to disappoint people, especially if they loved the little feathered fellow, as so many did. Roscoe had hundreds of loyal loving fans and friends, who only got a small taste of him through my internet postings, and I want to give them as much of the experience of living with him that I had. Sadly, one of those posts eventually led to the end of our times together. But even if I'd known what the future would bring, I still would have had to share his stories because he was simply too wonderful and so much fun that it would have been selfish to not share him with the world. Some treasures are not meant to be hoarded.

SPOILER ALERT! In case you didn't know or hadn't figured it out, Roscoe was: 1) a bird, 2) a male and 3) a Cardinal.

He was also my very special little friend.

During his time with me, I posted many stories of him on Facebook and other sites related to Cardinals. Sometimes it was to express my frustration and anger when caring for him was especially challenging. More were to tell the joy and wonder he brought into my life. Raising him was a special privilege and I wanted to be generous for those who could not actively participate. He brought me laughter, fascination and pride mixed with sorrow and pain. (And a good supply of bird droppings). Facebook was where so many people first met him and then shared the stories with their friends and family. Eventually there were people in North America, South America, Europe and Australia who were privy to his stories. I included a few of those Facebook posts at the end. These will include misspellings, crappy punctuation and autocorrect issues. This is to bring back your memories as best I can.

And to any doubters or naysayers, most of the stories I'm sharing here are backed up with photos or videos. Normally I have always been a "wish I'd thought to take a picture" kind of guy but I started recording my times with Roscoe at the beginning and my wife did as well. Today I cherish those videos and pictures as much as my son's baby pictures.

And so for all of his many fans, friends and supporters, this is for YOU! I hope you enjoy the stories and the memories. And because my wonderful wife, Grace, has always asked me to write a book about some of the crazy and weird experiences we have shared together, you will soon see I've taken a few side trips along the way to share a few of the more interesting or entertaining bits of our lives. So you're kind of getting a "two-fer".

And Roscoe was not the only bird who joined our family. There have been several and because the last one happened quite recently, I decided to toss them into the mix as well. So after we wrap up our Cardinal saga, I'll tell you about Fred, the Cockatiel and Jack Sparrow.

Introducing….Me!

Perhaps a quick introduction is called for. This is for the people who are reading this book, who are not familiar with me and my life. My name is Chip Kirkpatrick and my beloved wife, Grace and I live in Yulee, Florida. Yulee is a small area north of Jacksonville and west of Amelia Island / Fernandina Beach. It's a semi rural area and we have a house that sits on an acre of land placed on top of a bluff overlooking Lofton Creek and a wide expanse of marsh. It's a stunningly beautiful location with many large oak trees and a number of other ornamental and fruit trees, shrubs and bushes. When we bought the place in 2001, other than the trees there was little else by way of landscaping. So having a bit of a green thumb, I landscaped with butterflies and birds in mind. Living in Northeast Florida with it's mostly mild weather and with careful plantings, something is always flowering.

And something is always flying, fluttering, feeding or singing. It's a very active environment. I have placed a number of bird feeders and a couple of squirrel feeders around the property, mostly where we can observe our wild guests. An old hammock is hung near one of the squirrel feeders in the backyard and those bushy tailed rodents delight in running across it and making the fabric shimmer and dance. They especially enjoy jumping onto it from high in the nearby trees and trampolining on to or from the hanging feeder. They make meals more entertaining as we watch their antics from our dining room table. A small flock of chickens wander across the property, along with three cats. I always believed a landscape should incorporate color, action and song as well as horticulture.

I want the place where I live to have LIFE!

We have quite a menagerie of animals who share our bit of land with us. Alligators, otters and occasionally porpoises swim in the creek behind the house. Raccoons, possums, armadillos, rabbits, mice, rats, squirrels and bobcats prowl in the yard. Last year I put up security cameras and we are often surprised and delighted by our natural neighbors.

Reptiles and amphibians are well stocked too. Large numbers of tree frogs patrol our porch and bullfrogs line the marsh while toads guard the gardens. Skinks with their bright royal blue tails hide under flower pots or in the stack of firewood. And snakes! When we first bought the place I was mowing my lawn when I saw a snake slithering through the grass. I stopped and picked him up. It was a Ball Python, NOT a native species. It was somebody's lost pet and I took it around to all the neighbors and introduced myself and asked if they were missing a snake and presented it to them. NOBODY forgot me after this. The weird new guy with the snake was how I was often remembered. When nobody claimed him I released him in the rafters of my garage. The "slight rodent problem" we had disappeared. And after that whenever a neighbor finds a snake, they call me. I capture the poor reptile, thus preventing it's summary execution and take it to our yard and release it. (Probably every one of them promptly slithered right back to their old homes!)

And living on the water makes it even more special. I love to fish and the creek behind us is brackish water and numerous freshwater and saltwater species can be caught. Because we are on top of a bluff, the higher elevation gives us extended views and continual breezes which not only keep us cool but also blow away the mosquitoes and gnats that bother our neighbors. I am further blessed in regard to these flying razor blades as my poor wife must be much more tasty to them. She can slather on a thick coating of bug repellant and still they will cross the county line to attack her tender flesh. Meanwhile, I could be standing next to her buck naked and they will ignore me to attack her. But it <u>does</u> catch the neighbors' attention...

It's a wonderful place to live with a gorgeous view that goes for miles. We also experience magnificent sunrises and sunsets so our days begin and end with breathtaking vistas. A friend calls our place "The Estate" which delights my wife. Heaven can hardly be better than our home. Several times a day, I thank God for leading us to it and allowing us to live here.

Let's begin our saga...

What Have I Done?

May 12, 2018

The day after my 66th birthday. My buddy, MV Belyeu came up from Jacksonville to visit and he, Grace and I went into Fernandina Beach for breakfast. MV and I had worked together for a number of years and a friendship developed. MV was often shy and did not have many friends which was a shame because he was highly intelligent with a great sense of humor. He loved our place and said it was his favorite place on earth. He enjoyed fishing from our dock or just soaking in the breezes coming across the marsh. He'd nap in the hammock or simply sit quietly in one of the front porch rocking chairs with his eyes closed and a smile on his face. He and I would discuss the business of the world or just sit quietly enjoying each other's company. And he and Grace adored each other. A good friend.

MV also enjoyed a free meal and knew we were always happy to buy him a good breakfast from one of the local restaurants. He was one of our favorite people, so it was a worthwhile trade off. Coming back from breakfast that morning, I was sitting in the front seat next to him and was half facing him as we talked. Without warning he slams on the brakes and his Tahoe comes to an almost immediate halt. My seatbelt prevented me from flying into the dashboard or windshield (wear those seatbelts, people!) and possibly breaking my collarbone or my neck! Then MV raises his arm and points his finger ahead of us and asks "WHAT IS THAT?"

My eyes follow his finger and about 60 feet ahead of us is a small creature, jumping up and down in a circle in the middle of the road. Small and dark, my first thought was it was a toad or possibly a mouse. But neither species is known for standing and jumping on its rear legs, except in Disney films. Puzzled, I slipped from the car and walked up to it.

It was a bird. A tiny bird. A tiny bird that had no feathers on about a third of its body. A baby bird. A hatchling.

And I realized it was jumping up and down because the hot asphalt was burning its tiny feet and it could not figure out how to escape the pain.

I quickly knelt and scooped it up with both hands to get it off of the road. It began to struggle fiercely so I held it against my chest with one hand and with the other I tucked its wings and legs under my fingers so it couldn't move. Once that was done it settled down immediately. I studied it and saw there were no feathers on top of its head, around its face, on its neck and chest and around the wings and legs. The feathers it did have were a combination of black and grey. Two bright black eyes stared up at me.

I immediately thought to myself "**WHAT HAVE I DONE?**" The experts say to not touch baby birds but I doubt they took one being in the middle of a road into account. I slowly stood up, holding my prisoner with one hand and keeping the other free to ward off any attacks by angry parents. The bird looked like a Mockingbird or possibly a Blue Jay and both species are known to be territorial and very protective of their young. All of our cats sport bald spots on top of their heads from tangling with Mockingbirds by wandering too close to a nest. Mockingbirds have no fear and are often seen chasing hawks many times their size away from their territories. I braced myself for an angry parent to divebomb me but looking around frantically, I saw nothing.

RATS! If I had been attacked, I would have known the parents were nearby and would probably protect and feed their hatchling. And I might be able to locate the nest and return him to the relative safety of it. Without parental controls, I was likely to be totally responsible for this situation.. This rescue was starting off on a bad foot.

There was only one tree on the right side of the road and I headed towards it. It was only a few feet from the road but my heart sank as I approached it. The foliage was thin and I could tell there was no nest in it nor other birds within its branches.

I then looked at the ground and the nearby areas and realized I couldn't leave him there. There was an excellent chance he would soon be back on the road and the next driver may not have MV's reflexes or concern. There was little shade, no concealment nor food nor water. And he would be an easy target for a wide number of predators: dogs, cats, snakes, hawks, raccoons and possums. All live in the area and all would relish an easy snack.

Next I looked across the road.There was an ideal area to leave him where he might be able to survive. A number of trees, bushes and undergrowth would offer concealment and the possibility of food. If his parents could find him they might be able to protect and nurture him.

But all of this possibility was about 50 to 60 feet away from the road and between me and it was a well built barbed wire fence. In my younger years I possibly could have handled scaling the fence with minimal damage to my body but not while holding a baby bird. Even with two free hands, I knew my limits. I briefly considered throwing him towards the trees but I couldn't justify it in the hopes of him landing safely in one..

My first option was a wash out. Unless I was willing to simply leave him to his fate, which would be a bloody, painful demise of being torn apart and eaten alive, then I needed another option.

My next option was equally bad: Take him home and try and raise him.

NO! NADA! NOPE! NYET!

On a couple of previous occasions I had tried unsuccessfully to save orphaned / lost birds. One was a Blue Jay, which we named BLUE JAY LENO and then a Mourning Dove we called DOVE LETTERMAN, both after the late night talk hosts. Both birds were older, larger, and healthier than this very small bird. Sadly, neither bird would eat for me no matter what I tried and they both died after a couple of days. I felt so guilty after they died because I could not save them. I was not eager to relive those failures.

But the worst was Rocky.

Rocky was a baby flying squirrel and was named for Rocky / Rocket J Squirrel, of the cartoon duo Rocky and Bullwinkle, my favorite cartoon characters while I was growing up.

We found Rocky on a Friday evening. One of our cats brought the infant to us and dropped it at my feet.He was tiny, blind and mostly hairless. Likely he was merely hours old. I doted on him throughout the weekend. I placed him on a heating pad to keep him warm and gave him sips of a milk based concoction I made up with an eyedropper. Now remember all this was long before the Internet and Google and information was hard to come by. Somehow we managed to keep him alive Saturday and Sunday.

But Monday was coming! I would have to go to work!

Now I dreaded most Mondays anyway. I was a mid level manager for a Fortune 500 company for 32 years and my life had plenty of stress. Ours was a sales environment with sales objectives, customer issues, planning and preparations and much more and now I had the challenge of what can I do with this little helpless creature. Warmth and regular feedings were a necessity to keep him alive but I was frequently scrambling to keep up with my daily responsibilities and he was a major distraction. If I left him at home, unattended, he would certainly be dead when I returned. I could not leave the heating pad on for fear of causing a fire and he would need his regular feedings. What to do?

In desperation I came up with a plan.

I had a tiny rodent that needed constant food and warmth. I also had a job with a boss who would see no humor in me bringing Rocky with me. The last time I checked there was no NATIONAL BRING YOUR RODENT TO WORK DAY. I racked my brain for a possible solution. Maybe I could leave him in my car during the day and sneak out to feed him as often as possible. That would not work because the weather was cold and he must be kept warm. Plus my chain of slipping out of the office would eventually be noticed and eyebrows would be raised, questions would be asked and I doubted my explanation would be appreciated.

I did not know anybody I could trust to care for him properly and Grace also had a job, so the responsibility was fully mine.

Eventually, I had a plan. I typically wore a white long sleeve dress shirt, tie, and suit to work. So my plan was to line my breast pocket of my shirt with white toilet paper and place Rocky inside and put a bit of more paper on top of him. He should be invisible to a casual observer and my body heat should keep him warm and as long as he remained silent and still probably nobody would suspect he was there. And occasionally I would sneak out to the mensroom and enter a stall and slip him some formula to eat.

In retrospect, this was a horribly stupid plan. I was risking my career for a flying squirrel. Not a smart trade off. He didn't move nor squeak much but he was inclined to do both occasionally and either could alert someone to his presence. In my plan I hoped to isolate myself and stay in my office and avoid the other employees. I had an important project that was approaching its deadline and I would use that as my excuse to avoid everybody. Out of sight, out of mind.

I arrived at work early as I did most mornings. The office manager tended to stay isolated in his office during the day and my odds of avoiding him were 50/50. My job at this time was as the regional manager for a new line of products and my responsibilities included training and developing the sales reps in these products and planning and developing strategies to meet the corporate sales objectives. Because this was a brand new project, my territory was massive because there were only 6 managers handling a 9 state region and my area was about double the size of land and number of sales people than some of my co-workers. During most days, I normally rode on accounts with the outside salespeople, assisting them in making sales or rectifying client issues. But I pretty much controlled my own work schedule and a day or two in the office would not raise any eyebrows. When everything was in order in my office, I took off my suit coat because the office was unusually warm, then headed to the mens room. I wanted to feed Rocky before the workday went into full swing, to hold him over until I could do it again later in the morning. I stopped at the water fountain for a quick sip of water before entering the mens room when I felt a firm grip on my elbow that spun me around.

It was my boss. (In actuality he was not my true boss. My actual boss was at headquarters, 500 miles away. However my position and those like it had what was called a "dotted line" relationship to the local management in our respective areas. I served three different districts at that time which later was expanded to five and so it required a great deal of flexibility. He was the local sales manager in my primary district and I assisted him and his local teams and generally acquiesced to his requests. However I nearly always set my own schedules, training programs and worked as independently as possible.)

He had a frantic look on his face and he whispered loudly that I needed to go straight to the conference room. It seemed we had an unexpected visitor from headquarters to resolve an urgent issue. He was trying to gather the other members of the management team but it was still early and so far I was the only one he had found. I told him I had to go back to my desk first and he insisted I go straight to this meeting. If I had known what was coming my way I would have insisted or at least waited until his back was turned and tried to sneak back. However I have always tried to follow orders so I walked down the hall away from my desk. Very uncertain about what was happening I entered the conference room. The man I saw sitting at the table made my stomach churn.

OH SHIT!!!! IT WAS OUR CORPORATE VICE PRESIDENT!!!

Now normally I had gotten along with a long string of upper management as they changed fairly frequently within our organization, but this subhuman disliked me tremendously. And the feeling was mutual! In reality he did not get along with anybody in our organization. He had spent a period of time as our regional vice president before apparently Satan, himself, promoted him to corporate vice president and he moved to Atlanta where our headquarters were located. There was not a wet eye in the building the day he left! I was not alone in my feelings of celebration for his departure.

The man simply had no social skills. He rarely smiled and never laughed at jokes nor told any. He never greeted people as he passed them in the hallways nor did he acknowledge them. He was cold and unfriendly, unlike all of the other leadership.

He did have children so I must assume he was friendly with his wife. At least occasionally.

To give an example of his inability to relate or get along with his subordinate workers during his time with us locally, consider this: Anytime someone got on the elevator with him, he immediately put on a show of reading his messages on his Blackberry. But the entire management team also had them and we knew the contraptions did NOT work in the elevators, so he was staring at a blank screen. It was one of his ways of avoiding any human contact with the people who reported to him. When one of his immediate team members retired, he surprised everybody by showing up at the retirement party, where he congratulated and shook the hand of THE WRONG MAN! Yep, he mistook a complete stranger for the one who had reported directly to him for nearly a year! The retiree was standing next to him when he made the mistake. In fact he had to reach across the retiree to shake the wrong man's hand. Eyes were rolling everywhere as he tried to shrug the incident off. The following week, one of our salespeople also retired and again he surprised everybody by showing up at her party. But then he did not surprise anybody when he made a one minute speech where he announced that he didn't have to know the woman's name nor what she looked like. All he needed to know was that she had given the company 20 years of loyal service. Eyes were again rolling among the crowd as he said that and puzzled looks were exchanged. I have never heard a more desperate nor convoluted speech in all of my life. What a jackass!

But I am quite sure his dislike for me was a couple of notches higher than for others. When he first came to our organization as the regional vice president, he held a staff meeting and announced he wanted me to work on a "special project" starting the next day. I was the regional manager for a new product the company was launching and I had a very large geographical area to support covering about 60% of Florida. I supported several hundreds of salespeople and managers and had an extremely full schedule. But he insisted I travel 200 miles the next day to another office of his and work on this project with a second manager. I quickLy realized he had no idea of the costs this project would require and that my team had already done 2 versions of this idea. He wanted me to make the drive, spend 2 days on it and then present it to him the second afternoon. I did as requested and then on the second day he cancelled the afternoon meeting at the last minute and rescheduled it for the following week. I would again have to change my calendar and commitments for the following week in order to meet his schedules.

In reality I did not actually report to any of the local management but as I stated previously my position had a "dotted line" relationship to this man and his team of area sales managers. It made it a very challenging job as none of the regional teams worked together with the others and I was often asked to be in several locations, several hours of driving apart and doing different jobs all at the same time. Luckily I was able to coordinate things pretty well, but dealing with him was a difficult challenge. He had no concerns for my true job requirements nor any respect for what I did.

His rescheduling caused an issue with plans the local sales manager had scheduled for the following week. I explained the problem to the local Poobah and that I would not be available to meet his needs. He told me to not worry and to plan on being there for him because he would go to his new boss and clear the way for me to avoid the additional travel and meeting. The local sales manager then, acting as an intermediary between us, botched up the communications to me with the new altered plans. He basically left out one tiny but critical bit of the plans for my rescheduled meeting with The Big Guy. I was told he would want me to be available that day for a phone call at 2:00 pm to answer any questions he may have. No problem. I scheduled my day to be available for an hour starting at 2:00pm as requested. The rest of the day was having me ride with sales reps to see clients which was considered to be my primary responsibility. Then I could assist in selling our products or help resolve any client problems or complaints. And there was a major account with some serious issues that I needed to resolve. Surely an hour would give me ample time to answer any questions the VP may have because the project he was so in love with was fairly simple and I had a very strong suspicion that after he learned a bit more about what his "stroke of genius" would require it was likely he would change his mind on the whole thing. But until that point, I had to play my role.

That fateful morning, on my way out of the building with the sales rep, he was on the elevator with us. He asked what my plans were and I confidently outlined my day with the clients we were scheduled to see. He asked if I would be available to call him at 2:00 as planned and I assured him I would. He seemed satisfied and wished us a productive day.

As promised, I called promptly at 2:00. His secretary told me he was in a meeting and put me on hold. Ten minutes later she picked up and told me he would call me back in a couple of minutes. I asked her to remind him I had a sales call scheduled at 3:00 with a major account. She said she would tell him. He called me back at 2:50 and politely asked if I had time to talk to him and I told him yes but we needed to talk quickly as the rep and I were about to enter the client's office. He seemed surprised and asked if I was going on sales calls. I reminded him that I was and had told him that in the elevator, but what questions did he have and I would try to give him the answers. Instead he calmly told me to not bother but to go and see the client. I again asked what questions he had but again he told me to not worry about them and wished us a good sales call. I hung up.

Around 7pm I was preparing to go home when the local sales manager stormed into my office screaming how dare I refuse to work with the VP?

The maniac on the fourth floor had just chewed this manager out, telling him I had stood him up on our telephone call and disrespected him by refusing to assist with his plan! I was shocked and confused. I carefully explained what had transpired in the elevator and that I had promptly called him at the specified time. I then covered what had happened and how the VP seemed ok with what was happening and dismissed me from the call even after I insisted I could speak with him before keeping our scheduled sales call. Luckily the sales rep I was working with that day was still in the office and verified what I said and done. Then I saw a look of realization come over the manager's face and only then did he tell me the VP had been expecting me to be available for a two hour conference call with him and he had omitted that detail in his instructions to me. Nor had the VP mentioned it during our elevator ride when I had outlined my schedule for the day. The impression I had been given was to be available to answer any questions he may have on the proposal and I had assumed an hour would be sufficient for that. Plus the VP failed to keep his appointment with me! And of course he had stood me up at the secondary office. Well the sales manager promised to go immediately to explain my innocence in the issue and put me back in his good graces. However, after he left me, he realized his mistake would not be well received and would reflect poorly on him and he simply lacked the courage to admit it was his error. I was left "dangling in the wind". I did not learn of this betrayal for quite a while and then the VP refused to discuss it with me.

Our conversation in the elevator that morning was the last time he ever spoke civilly to me.

As I stated before, I was more of a support person at that time reporting to a different management team, but in the corporate world there are straight lines and dotted lines of responsibility that merge and confuse issues and the general rule is if your office is high enough at headquarters, EVERYBODY reports to you. So I was royally screwed.

So now I am trapped in a room with him and an unpredictable squirrel is in my clothing. Worse, I was obligated to sit across from him at the table and then try to make small talk. He was horrible at small talk but great at ignoring people. I quickly gave up trying to be polite. Instead I adopted his tactic and pretended I was working on various projects. In reality I was mentally trying to find an escape from the meeting and the room. Never before had I wished that someone would call me to report my house was on fire or an obscure family member had just died.

Finally the rest of the group entered and he began his spiel. Apparently we had a local problem and he had flown down from Headquarters in the hopes of resolving the crisis. I think we were in there for at least three hours but I do not recall. The entire episode was a blur of fear and panic. All Rocky had to do was stretch or change position and my horrible secret would be revealed. A single cry of hunger or discomfort and I would be crying with him as I exited the building for the last time. My career was possibly dissolving with every second that passed.

I'm pretty sure I was asked for an opinion or to answer a question but since I have no recollection of what we were discussing I can't imagine I added to the conversation or helped reach a solution.

Eventually we were excused and we dispersed. Hopefully I did not knock anybody down during my frenzied exit from the room. I made a beeline for the stairs and plunged downward constantly saying ***"THANKYOUGODTHANKYOUGODTHANKYOUGOD!"***. Two floors down an outside company leased the entire floor and I exited. I had no business there but I quickly found myself in the last stall of their mensroom and I then gingerly pulled out the toilet paper, marvelling that Rocky had managed to stay still and silent for so long. A miracle had happened. My career was safe.

Moments later I realized why he had been so cooperative. He had joined Jay and Dove on my list of orphan rescue failures.

Quietly I wrapped him in toilet paper and gave him a burial at sea.

So this was why I did not want to take this little bird home. A bit of me died with the other three and I didn't care to see it happen again.

OPTION 2 was a washout.

I stood there thinking as hard as I could. Leaving him would result in his death and likely a suffering one. The heat, lack of food and water, and the inevitability of being eaten alive were all too horrible to consider. But taking him with me would likely result in a painful death by starvation since I was not successful in feeding the others, I had no reason to expect to do any better this time.

And then I considered Option 3. Option 3 offered many benefits for both of us. It would shorten the outcome and prevent much of the pain and suffering he was likely to experience. All I would need to do would be to place him gently on the ground and raise my right leg. I would smash him over and over again with my foot until there was nothing but a puddle of goo and a few feathers. Likely he would die with the first strike.

His suffering would be over. BUT mine would only be beginning. There was no doubt that I would vomit for 2 days and have nightmares and bad memories for the rest of my life. I'm simply not cut out for this kind of thing.I have a strong appreciation of the value of life. As an example I love to fish but generally release my catches. I capture spiders, flies, even roaches that enter into our home and release them outside. I'd probably be a great Buddhist.

Too bad I'm not a vegan but no sense in going overboard!

I looked down at my tiny prisoner. He was so little, so young. He was ugly as sin without his feathers but there was a sense of dignity there. And those black eyes. They were bright when I captured him but now there was a sadness or a sense of resignation in them. I have no idea what other species may know or understand about life and death but it appeared he realized the end was near and he was preparing himself for whatever his immediate future would bring.

That made my decision for me.

I marched to MV's vehicle and climbed inside. The prisoner was still securely in my grasp. From the backseat Grace calmly asked, "What are you going to do with <u>THAT</u> ?"

"What Are You Going To Do With <u>THAT</u>?"

was Grace's question, but I heard the amusement in her voice. After nearly 45 years together, she is generally on my wavelength and vice versa. It's eerie when one of us says the exact words the other was preparing to say. She knows what I will do or say before I do and so she was not surprised when I returned to the car with company. "I have no idea", I replied.

"Ok!" was all she said in response. This was nothing new to her. She is well used to my eccentricities.

Minutes later we arrived at home. MV said his goodbyes and we entered our house. I grabbed my iPad and entered Google in the hopes of finding what care a baby bird requires. Meanwhile Grace was looking for something to put our visitor in so I could regain use of my second hand.

While I was scanning the internet I dialed our local bird rescue. Their line was busy so I hung up. I immediately redialed and now the phone rang and rang. After 20 rings I hung up and redialled. Again it rang repeatedly. How could they get away from the telephone so quickly? It was only a few seconds between the busy signal and the unanswered ringing. A few more unsuccessful attempts to contact them I simply let the telephone ring. Several minutes and dozens of rings later an answering machine picked up. The message was basically that they were in a busy time of year and likely assisting birds in the field and I should leave a detailed message. It ended with a sincere sounding promise to call back as soon as possible. I left a very detailed message that basically was I had an infant bird and was trying to save it but needed their vast experience and knowledge on how to care for it. I tried to make it clear that I was not trying to dump the little fellow on them to care and raise. I was willing to do whatever was necessary myself. I simply needed a little advice on what to do.

Then I played my Ace card.

I mentioned my brother, Mike. Mike had done a great deal of volunteer work for them for several years, such as finding and capturing reported injured birds of prey and transporting them to the Center. He cleaned pens and did yard work and other scut duties. He also raised and released a number of orphaned raccoons and once a baby otter that had been brought to them. Ozzie, the otter, was an interesting experience for my brother. The little fellow slept with my 10 year old nephew and soon was more of a dog than an otter. He would walk beside you without a leash or collar. Once we took him to the Sante Fe River to see if he was ready and willing to return to the wild. But as we swam and dove, he stayed beside us. My brother had a chocolate Labrador Retriever and another neighbor had one too. The three became a pack and roamed the neighborhood. They swam in the creek behind the houses and would take a dip in peoples' pools. Everybody loved the threesome because Ozzie was so friendly. He would run up to everybody hoping to have his ears scratched or his head patted.

There was only one person who wasn't totally happy to have an otter as a neighbor. Otters are very particular about where they relieve themselves. They will pick one particular spot that is a short distance away from their den, or in this case, house. And they will return there faithfully to do their business. Well Ozzie picked a spot that did not meet with the approval of this particular neighbor. When Mother Nature called, he would run three houses away where the people had a screened in porch. There was a tear in the screening and he would slip through to a small wrought iron table and chair set. He would hop up on the chair and then on top of the table where he would deposit his dietary leftovers. Since otters eat primarily fish this would be a very unpleasant and smelly surprise for the owners to find. The man complained several times to my brother about having to hose out his screened porch on a daily basis. But finally he admitted that he really enjoyed the other parts of Ozzie's visits and if it really bothered him that much he could finally fix the tear in the screen.

The saga of Ozzie came to an end when my brother's alarm system in his house mysteriously went off one day. The police were sent and nobody was home, so they made a courtesy walk around the house. There was a dog pen that Ozzie was supposed to stay in but he was easily able to slip out and generally did so he could roam the neighborhood with his 2 doggy pals. But on this particular day he had stayed inside of it. When my brother came home from work that evening there was a Florida Wildlife Commission truck parked in the driveway. Ozzie was in a cage in the back and an officer was waiting with a pair of handcuffs, prepared to arrest my brother. Apparently it is against state laws to keep many animals, a fact I was to learn in more detail years later and the penalties can be quite severe. Quickly my brother explained how he had acquired Ozzie and the officer put the handcuffs away. However he informed my brother that he was confiscating Ozzie because my brother did not have a permit to keep the animal. Mike replied he believed he was working under the umbrella of the organization's permit. The officer strongly informed Mike that he could not keep the animal under the organization's permits and he would need his own and he would NEVER be issued a permit. The State of Florida simply did not want its wildlife kept in captivity and strictly limited who was allowed to be granted the necessary permits. To be given permits required a great deal of study and education.

My brother and my nephews wept as Ozzie was driven away.

Ozzie eventually was put in a zoo in Orlando and he lived with several other otters in a big enclosure. The nephew who slept with Ozzie often drove down to check on him. He would call my brother and then put his cell phone on speaker. My brother had a special whistle he would do at feeding time and he would whistle into the phone. Suddenly Ozzie would stop whatever he might be doing and would look around searching. Then he would spot my nephew and would run or swim to him and would try to get to him through the fence or glass barriers. Clearly he had not forgotten his previous life nor his earlier family.

A couple of years ago they learned that Ozzie had died. He was 16 years old. My brother still misses Ozzie.

Years later I would have my own run in with the Florida Wildlife Commission.

I waited several hours before calling the bird rescue center again and leaving the same message. But this time I reminded them that I had also tried to be of assistance to the center. On several occasions I had made the hour and a half drive to their location to deliver fresh fish and fish offal for them to use to feed their hawks, owls, ospreys and eagles. One trip included a 17 pound channel catfish that should have fed a large number of birds and maybe provided a few fried fish dinners for the staff. And hours later they received a third message. No response.

Meanwhile I saw on the internet that canned cat food with the gravy or oil removed would sustain my feathered buddy. Likewise dry cat food soaked in water for several hours would work. But it also cautioned NOT to give them water. Apparently they are susceptible to drowning if given too much water. I began soaking some dry food and collected some of the wet food from our cats' bowl and started scraping the gravy from a can of Purina shreds.

Then Grace appeared from our garage bearing a small cardboard box and a small woven basket. PERFECT! The basket greatly resembled a nest and was nearly a perfect size. She lined it with paper towels to more closely resemble a nest. The basket also had a handle that looped over it which would become a perfect platform for feeding and for him to sleep on when he got a little older. The basket fit neatly inside the box which was deep enough to momentarily keep him inside.

Again having two hands to work with I made preparations to feed the intruder. I took newspaper into our sunroom and spread it on our coffee table and then brought the food (scraped wet cat food) and finally our reluctant guest.

Since much of this book takes place in our sunroom, let me share a few details about it..

It is 12'x20'. It is situated at the rear of our house in the southeast corner. Both the eastern and southern sides are mostly windows with a 2 foot border at the top and bottom of the walls. A glass security / storm door opens onto a small deck and stairway leading to the backyard. The two non-glass walls are paneled with unfinished cypress. There is a door on both of these walls, one leads to the livingroom and the second, a set of double doors, into our bedroom. A third door goes to our backyard which has a number of large oak trees. Beyond them is a steep dropoff of about 30 feet to Lofton Creek. A very steep stairwell goes to our small dock. The water here is brackish, dark, swift and very deep. Both freshwater and saltwater fish can be caught from the dock. The creek is over 100 feet across and a marsh begins on the opposite bank. The creek weaves through the marsh like a snake. A straight line course is approximately 6 miles to the Nassau River but the waterway is over 26 miles by boat to reach that same spot. We enjoy truly spectacular sunrises and sunsets when the marsh grasses turn to gold and the skies become a brilliant red, pink, purple and finally a brilliant blue.

When we first married we had plans to buy property on the water in Florida and property in the Blue Ridge Mountains of North Carolina. We would build identical log homes on the properties and even furnish them the same. Then when we retired we would spend six months at one and six months at the other. Since everything would be the same it would be as if we hadn't actually changed locations. Eventually we abandoned the idea as impractical. However the treeline across the marsh resembles the foothills of North Georgia and our house resembles a log home and so Grace brags it's as if we actually had our two dream properties. I agree.

I was a dedicated fisherman and the paneled walls of the sunroom are decorated with numerous fishing plaques, artwork and assorted fishing related items . A 6 horsepower Johnson motor hangs on one wall. This was purchased by my father, two weeks after I was born. In the corner of the two interior walls is a bright red leather recliner. Beside it is a pole lamp. The southern wall has a leather loveseat and a matching pair of granite topped end tables flank it. In front of the loveseat is a matching coffee table. The tables hold gooseneck lamps and Grace's African Violets. A ceiling fan and lamps are overhead and a woven indoor/outdoor rug pulls it all together.

Our property is marked on maps as Henry's Landing. It was a popular place for locals and South Georgians to come and party, fish, crab, cook and camp. Rumor is somebody drove a VW into the creek. All I can say is I have retrieved auto parts while fishing so maybe the story is true. Also the first man executed by the electric chair in Florida, dumped his wife's body near us and she was found floating where my dock is. The next day they found her mother a half mile away.

In spite of its bloody past, it is a wonderful place. Beautiful, peaceful and teeming with wildlife.

I have invested a lot of time and effort into the landscaping. My goal was to make it butterfly and hummingbird friendly. I selected numerous flowering shrubs and bushes with the goal of always having something in bloom. In addition to the large majestic oaks that were here I have added around 50 flowering and fruit trees and likewise for the bushes and shrubs. I have placed 11 bird feeders in the front yard and 3 in the backyard as well as 7 bird baths and watering stations. A wide variety of bird houses and a bat house offers additional protection and reproduction opportunities. But the semi-natural environment brings birds by the hundreds. Perfect for any bird watchers and lovers.

I didn't forget our squirrels either. I have a large metal feeder that hangs from a chain from a large oak in the backyard. This is for the squirrels and they flock to it. It is placed in the center of our window view in the living / dining room. Their antics running up and down the chain are wonderful but I had placed a woven hammock between two trees beside the feeder. Time and weather has deteriorated it where I wouldn't dare recline in it. But it's a perfect squirrel trampoline. They will leap onto it and catapult onto the feeder or simply bounce around on it. Mostly we can not actually see them as they play on it but we can track their movements from the underside of the hammock where it curves up to the trees.

Hilarious

This is the world we brought our little friend into. We thought the sights of the outside world from the windows would be beneficial for him. He could watch the other birds and hear their songs. Maybe he wouldn't feel so lonely.

Hummingbirds, Sparrows, Wrens, Finches, Robins, Jays, Red Winged Blackbirds, Bluebirds, Hawks, Ospreys, Mockingbirds, Woodpeckers and Cardinals live here all year long. Migrating flocks of other species find us a place to stop, feed, rest and prepare for their northern or southern journey.

And so I brought our guest into this room and I placed some newspaper on the coffee table and then I sat on the tile floor with my legs beneath it. I placed the prepared foods nearby and gently reached into the box and pulled the basket out. He looked up warily at me and when I offered a morsel of gourmet baby bird food on the tip of my finger, he turned his head away.

Sighing, I had flashbacks to the jay and dove and how they refused my efforts to save their lives. I tried again and again and he rebuffed me each time and hopped away. Gritting my teeth I reached in and captured him in my hand. He squawked loudly in protest and struggled to get away. I again tucked his extremities into the confines of my hand and he stopped his protests.

Again, I managed to position a morsel on the tip of a finger and offered it to him. He turned his head. I had a thought that his parents must have taught him the "STRANGER! DANGER!" concept of avoiding contact with unknown personages and I silently congratulated them on the effectiveness of their teachings. He wanted nothing to do with me. Already in my head I was digging another tiny grave in the yard.

If I had been born with a third arm, hand and fingers this would have been easy.

 A third hand could pry his tiny beak open allowing me to stuff him with nutritious foods. Without that I realized I was hopelessly outnumbered by a small ball of feathers and fluff.

Finally I turned to desperation. Everything I read said don't give them water. There's no explanation why but this gave me a "Hail Mary" move to try. We had a syringe so I took some of the discarded cat food gravy and mixed it with water, thinning it to a consistency that would pass through the small opening of the syringe.I then pulled some of it into the syringe and as I held him I squirted a few drops on the side of his beak. No response. My magic concoction simply ran down the side of his beak onto my fingers. I did it again. NADA! A third time and some must have leaked in because I saw his beak move rapidly up and down and then saw him swallow. I did it again and again and he became slightly more willing to accept it. Finally I think he had his fill and I stopped. Either he was thirsty, hungry or afraid that I intended to drown him a few drops at a time. And the real question was if I was actually accomplishing anything? Was he taking in bits of nutrients or poison? Maybe I was advancing his end instead of preventing it. I watched carefully for signs of spasms or trembling or pain. Instead he seemed sleepy. I carefully put him inside of the basket and tucked more paper towels around him to keep him warm and tip toed out of the room.

It was 10:45am. The texts all said he needed to be fed every 15 minutes. EVERY FIFTEEN MINUTES???? No way.

I tiptoed back in after an hour and saw he was awake. I held him and the battle restarted. He would not accept the solid foods I offered. Soon I had reconstituted cat food on my hands and arms all the way to the elbow. It was on my shirt and pants and all over the spots of the table I had not covered. I looked carefully at the ceiling, certain there would be tiny stalagmites of this mess. He wore a small helmet on his head of dried cat food and it was caked on his beak, chest and face. Finally I brought out the syringe again and eventually he took a few sips. But not willingly!

This was our routine for the day. Every hour or so I fought against his apparent desire to starve to death. There was no doubt in my mind that he was willing to die just to humiliate me. Once he opened his beak, just a bit. Perhaps he needed to sneeze or cough or simply yawn but sensing an opportunity, I went for it! Full speed ahead! Damn the torpedoes! I managed to get the syringe into his beak and squirted a tiny morsel inside and he looked shocked and insulted. I held his head upward and stroked his throat until I felt him swallow.

He gave me a very very dirty look. Apparently I wasn't playing fair.

And so I spent my day being a bird's wetnurse. Tiny bits here. A sip of watered down gravy there. Over and over and over. I was frustrated, angry and saddened over my apparent failures. He didn't seem to care.

I went to bed that first night with a strong foreboding of another disaster coming my way.

The Second Morning

I awoke early the second morning and went into the sunroom to check on our uncooperative guest. I peeked into the box where his little basket sat and was expecting and hoping to see a pair of shiny black eyes peering up at me. Instead I saw a motionless little body laying inside the basket, partially covered by the paper towels lining it. I whispered "Good morning" but there was no response. I repeated it much louder. Nothing. I even sang a silly little tune that became his Good Morning song every morning we were together. It went like this to the tune of the Happy Birthday song:

"Good morning to you!

Good morning to you!

Good morning little twerp bird (or whatever message I wanted to convey to him!)

GOOD MORNING TO YOUUUUUUUUUUUU!" (It was sung loudly and off key).

There was no reaction. No movement! No putting his wings over his ears to block the horrible sound.

Nothing.

A feeling of foreboding and doom crept over me. I picked the basket up and brought it closer so I could see the contents more clearly. There was no sign of life. He was still and appeared to be stiff from rigor mortis.

I sighed heavily but was not surprised. The odds of pulling him through were strongly against me and the bird. I was momentarily angry. First at him for dying on me and then against myself for so stupidly "trying to play God". I had already failed 3 times and apparently I am a slow learner.

The only thing left to do was to wrap the tiny corpse into some paper towels and dig a grave in one of the gardens. And I wanted to do it before Grace woke.

I slipped on my shoes, took a couple of paper towels and picked up the body. Suddenly a bloodcurdling scream erupted from the bird and a microsecond later one came out of me! I certainly wasn't expecting that reaction! It's not often I resurrect the dead.

HE WAS STILL ALIVE! HE HAD SIMPLY BEEN ASLEEP!

He leapt up out of my hand and attempted to fly away but only traveled a foot or 2 before crashing to the floor. I took a few seconds to let my pulse drop down closer to normal before picking him up and returning him to his basket. I heard Grace, in the next room sleepily, ask if I was okay. Clutching my chest as my heart pounded furiously, I assured her that I was okay and she should go back to sleep.

Our second day together had begun…

My Time in Hell

I continued the fight to force feed a bit of nutrition into him. I fared no better than I had yesterday. Since I had not yet heard from the local bird rescue group, I started the second day by calling again. And again. And again. I left another message and I'm sure my growing exasperation and anger were evident in my voice tone. Then I searched the internet for bird or animal rescue organizations around me. There were about a dozen in Northeast Florida and Southeast Georgia. Some specified they catered to various species of mammals only, most were nonspecific. Eventually I called all of them within a 150 to 200 mile radius.

NOBODY ANSWERED! Every call resulted in long chains of telephone rings. Some went on unabated. Others finally would trigger a voicemail after dozens of rings. And all of those pre-recorded messages were virtually identical. "Sorry we aren't here to take your call. This is our busy season and we are probably busy helping some birds / animals!"

How about somebody helping THIS little fellow?

The next few hours are a blur to me now, but I remember flashes of anger, dismay, depression and overall feeling like a failure. This bird was going to die and all of my best efforts weren't going to prevent it. Since I was trying everything I could think of, I placed the blame squarely on the featherless head of this uncooperative little monster! On multiple occasions I felt like reverting back to OPTION 1 and driving him back to where we found him and leaving him to fend for himself. Even worse was when I fantasized about OPTION 3 and smashing him into a small puddle of goo and feathers. This occurred when it seemed he was intentionally trying to make me fail, even at the cost of his own life.

This must be a bird from Hell, sent to torment me. Perhaps I was actually dead and already suffering in invisible flames, doomed to try and get this stupid bird to eat for all of eternity.

No wait! I can't be in Hell because Grace is here with me! Anybody who meets my wife quickly realizes if there's a line to get past the Pearly Gates when she arrives, Saint Peter will personally escort her to the front of the line. She'd probably be allowed to cut in front of Mother Teresa and all of the Popes. Truly. She's that good, a wonderful, beautiful person. I'm very lucky that she is in my life.

I know. I know. You're wondering how I got her to marry ME! Well you'll have to buy another book to learn THAT secret.

Ok. So what is the problem here? You already know or at least suspect there is a happier ending than him suffering "Death by Nike" or becoming a snake snack.Well this was all his fault. And mine.

Initially I tried to get him to open his beak and let me cram something edible into his craw which he would obligingly swallow and then ask for more.

Nope. He had an irreversible case of lockjaw (lockbeak?).

I tried everything I could think of including the "Airplane Method" used on small humans ("BRRRRM! Here comes the airplane ready to land. Open up the hangar doors for him!"). Apparently he didn't like airplanes. My fingers began to cramp from struggling to balance those slimy bits of food. He seemed to have a death wish and it seemed like his wish might soon come true.

Like I said earlier I seriously questioned my sanity and intelligence in taking this project on. I was clearly outgunned and outmanned by this speck of a bird. And my frequent calls and voicemails to the local bird rescue were either ignored or unheeded which greatly added to my unhappiness and depression. Finally I started calling all of the rescue organizations again! I again left messages that I was desperately seeking just information on what to feed my orphan and how to care for it. I mean these were real Academy Award winning performances. I tried to make my voice break a little and maybe a few tears in the hopes that someone would take pity on me and call me back.

I had always considered myself to be a better than average actor and I threw every bit of emotion, sadness and desperation into the phone. Meryl Streep would have gnashed her teeth and pulled her hair out in professional envy if she had heard me. It's likely she would have left Hollywood and entered a nunnery after realizing that all of her many acting skills could not compete with me. Not even SOPHIE'S CHOICE came close.

But I had no audience.

It was 10 days before someone returned my calls! TEN DAYS! And it was NOT the local organization I called so many times but a mammal rescue group in Gainesville, Florida, about 80 miles away. The woman said she was simply wanting to confirm that somebody had called me and offered me some help. Before I could respond, she advised me there was a local person who cared for birds and started to give me their information and I stopped her and told her that I had already called numerous times with no response. And that she was the only response I had received. I did refrain from saying that after 10 days, a callback was of NO value to me, since had I not stumbled my way into a solution, the little fellow would have been long dead from starvation. I will not share her reaction to my news, but it wasn't pretty. She had a very strong grasp of the use of vulgarities and I frankly was a bit impressed. Her cursing wove a verbal tapestry that I've rarely heard the likes of in all my life. And I know some men who were masters of this type of vocabulary, but never a woman. Then the lady gave me what information she could and told me this time of year IS a very busy time for these people. Then she wished me good luck and hung up. I was once again alone but at this point I had apparently stumbled my way through.

NOTE: The next day I DID receive a call from the local facility and I'm pretty sure the Gainesville woman had likely reached them and probably again demonstrated her fluency in vulgar language. They were honest enough to say they weren't sure why they didn't call me sooner because they did receive my messages and they remembered my brother fondly for all the volunteer work he had done for them. It was again said it was a very busy time for them. Sadly they did not sound very sincere and I wondered why they bothered to call me.

I do NOT want this to sound like I'm bashing these people (too much). They are mostly unpaid volunteers who undertake a very arduous and occasionally dangerous mission. Often they pay for all supplies, foods, cages, medicines and other expenses from their own pockets or spend untold hours fundraising or begging for help. I was exasperated and a bit angry at this time but the amount of time, money and care I spent for ONE bird gives me greater respect for all of these folks who simply love God's creatures and try to help when and how they can.

So cut them some slack! And send them money. We actually put this group in our will, along with the Boy Scouts, Humane Society and a few other groups, whose work we respect and admire.

Midday was approaching and I tried unsuccessfully one more time to feed my unwanted guest and then placed him into the basket and tucked some paper towels around him to keep him warm. I put the basket into the box and turned off the overhead light. As I did I glanced into the box to see two tiny black eyes staring back at me. I again realized I was this tiny Child of God's only hope.

My heart broke. Likely he was screwed.

The Second Afternoon

(A Taste of Success)

I left him and went outside to finish a few chores and to eat lunch. Grace noted my sadness and having guessed the reason, so she tried to bolster my spirits by reminding me that he wasn't dead yet and if he died it would not be because I had walked away, leaving him to die. She has always had a wonderful grasp of The Big Picture of Life. It helped but only slightly.

After lunch, I decided to take another swipe at my mission. When I went into the sunroom, I found he was not nestled inside the basket but instead perched on top of the handle that formed a high loop above the rest of the basket. Inspired, I held my finger out to him and he obligingly stepped onto it. This was a very pleasant surprise but once I carefully lowered myself onto the floor and picked up a morsel of food and offered it to him he held his head back and opened his beak as wide as it could go!!!

I let out a shout to Grace to come quickly and this again sent him into a short aborted flight. But when I held my finger out to him he again returned to it. Grace came into the room and I excitedly told her what was happening. She sat in the recliner to watch the show..

But my excitement quickly faded as the battle went into a new phase.

Now this part is mostly MY fault. It seems his hunger made him willing to accept me as a substitute parent but circumstances were not in my favor. I don't know if all baby birds do this or if desperation to fill his belly caused him to do this but whenever I held food over his head his whole body would shake and quiver violently. I was trying to balance this goo on the tip of my finger so I could plunge it into his beak as a parent bird would thrust a bug or morsel with their beak, into their young's gullet. Unfortunately I was proving the existence of gravity over and over as any attempt to shove the food downward towards his innards resulted in the slimy morsel sliding off my finger and landing nowhere near the spot where I was intending to deposit it. It didn't help that he continued to shake, rattle and roll. It was like watching a severe case of St Vitus' Dance or a full body ephileptic fit. I have some severe vision issues including being legally blind in my left eye. This brings on depth perception problems and this compounded with a fear of hurting him, in addition to his vibrating stance, made me miss getting food to his beak most of the time. I had this baseless fear of stabbing the food into his beak with such force that I would literally tear the beak off from his head. There is an old black and white cartoon I saw as a child where this happened to a bird character and I think that has been embedded into my brain causing this foolish worry. In the cartoon, the bird's beak fell completely from his head into two pieces, the upper beak and the lower. The bird then simply snapped his beak back on, like an old man popping his dentures into his mouth. However I was pretty sure that would not happen in real life. That plus the sliminess of the morsels caused them to fall off of the tip of my finger prematurely so I was either coating the side of his head with a gooey pastelike mess or depositing a foodless finger into his maw.

It was like trying to land a fighter jet on the deck of a carrier in the middle of a hurricane at night while blindfolded. Very frustrating and frightening.

This is a common issue for new parents when trying to dress their first baby. I remember when our son, Chad was born and a nurse showed us how to dress him. She laughed and commented how it took two adults to dress a single baby. After watching us stumble and fumble, She took over and I watched helplessly as she bent his limbs into positions I would have sworn the human body could not tolerate without damage requiring much orthopedic care to correct. But miraculously he survived unscathed and eventually we also could dress him without injury or death. Although today at age 34, Chad is again a challenge for us to dress…

Likewise my care of this bird eventually had me shoving food into his gullet, driving my fingers so deep into his maw, I'd have sworn I tickled his large intestines.

But not at this time. Nope I was still being cautious and I paid the price. Frustration, anger, and despair welled up in me and soon I was cursing the bird for not being more cooperative and pliant. I cursed MV for stopping his car instead of flattening this little monster and rendering him into a small grease spot in the middle of the road.

But mostly I cursed myself. I knew I shouldn't get involved in hopeless situations like this, instead I should just look the other way and keep going. I shouldn't be so tenderhearted. Plenty of my friends would have recognized the futility of the situation and would have snuffed him out as a gesture of mercy, by ending its suffering or as a matter of convenience, because they have more important things to accomplish. Or simply because they would not care about his circumstances nor it's fate. I also cursed myself because of my eyesight problems and the difficulty it gives me. I cursed myself for being weak, for being stupid but mainly I cursed myself for being….me.

And Then It Happened!

Now the dried cat food I had soaked in water is made in the form of tiny fish and mostly I was breaking them up in order to make it easier for me to handle and also easier for him to swallow. But then I took a whole one and held it between 2 fingers by the "tail". I held it over his head and he lifted his head towards it and opened his beak. WIDE! Then, like Luke Skywalker rushing to fire his photon torpedo to destroy the Death Star, I went full speed ahead. Like a dive bomber intent on destroying its target, my finger aimed straight for that open beak. He stopped shaking and quivering for a moment, my vision cleared and the "fish" went into his beak. But this time I didn't yank my finger out, which often also pulled the food out of his mouth. No, this time I went deeper still, forcing the fake fish towards his throat. Then remembering the image of the beakless cartoon bird, I snatched my digit back. I watched with awe and wonder as he opened and closed his beak several times with the morsel still in place. I was afraid he was going to spit it out but he was merely adjusting the morsel to a better position. Then he raised his head until it was practically vertical, the fake fish slid deeper and he snapped his beak shut. I saw a couple of minor convulsions in his throat as he worked the tidbit downward and then he swallowed.

SWALLOWED!

The skies overhead cleared and I swear a band of angels sang the Hallelujah chorus. I could only stare at the minor miracle that just happened. I was in a state of shock and joy and I whispered to him , **"Way to go, Roscoe!"**

And then he had a name. Roscoe.

And I began to think I might pull this off.

He might live.

The Status Quo

Well you may think everything immediately improved, life became easier, I dropped 20 pounds, won the Lottery and World Peace broke out across the globe.

It didn't.

No he still was a challenge to feed but I didn't mind as much because I was now the Little Engine Who Could. I became more relaxed and wasn't so afraid of injuring him and while my lousy vision caused me to miss more than connect with his beak I no longer wanted to return him to where we found him nor smash his tiny body.

Or at least, not quite as much.

So gradually he began to sit on my finger and eat but before long he avoided my finger and stood on the coffee table.. There he continued to take food from me but quickly learned to pick it up from the table top, much as he would forage on the ground in the wild. And that was ok by me.

A New Development

After a few days, I left him sitting on the handle of the basket, inside the box while I tended to other business. An hour later I returned to feed him again, only to find the box was empty! I scanned the room but did not see him. I got down on hands and knees and crawled around the room, peering under the furniture and other items in the room but failed to find him. I got a flashlight to better illuminate under the furniture and in the corners and again crawled around trying to find him.Slightly alarmed I began moving furniture and checking behind the pillows on the loveseat and among the magazines and other knick knacks.

NO BIRD!

Now in a full scale panic mode I started racing around the room rechecking items but now mostly looking for a small pile of feathers which would indicate the previous owner no longer required them. Our 3 cats had shown a great interest in him, especially Sparky. First the sunroom had once been Sparky's favorite room and domain and now he was banned from it. Always warm and toasty with plenty of soft places to nap, it was his special domicile and no doubt he wondered why we blocked him from entering.

AND NOW THERE WAS A BIRD!

All of our cats are hunters and stalking birds is their favorite pastime. Sparky would often be on the landing outside of the sunroom when I fed Roscoe. Or he would be on the other side of the door leading to the living room. That door has a number of small windows but a sheer curtain blocks a direct view and shadows can easily be observed. He spent hours watching and waiting, looking for an opportunity.

I suddenly was very afraid that when I exited the room, one of the cats had slipped in unnoticed and had spoiled their dinner by having a snack first. They are quite capable of slipping into a room, unseen, as we slip out. And Sparky is especially skilled at this. He's not allowed in our bedroom and yet we often find him lounging on top of our pillows, merrily shedding his long silky hair. On MY pillow!

I saw no cat but if they could sneak IN when I exited, they could also sneak OUT when I reentered. Panic mode on HIGH, I screamed for Grace to come help me. Fearing I had suffered a heart attack, stroke, been attacked by a rabid bear or anally probed by space aliens or any of the other possibilities that entered her imaginative mind, she rushed into the room.

"I can't find Roscoe!" I screamed, "Help me look!"

She calmly pointed over my head and said, "He's up there."

I followed the direction of her upward jutting digit. Over the set of double French doors that lead to our bedroom, I have an old fishing rod and reel that hangs horizontally. Perched on the rod was my missing feathered youngster. For the first time I noticed that in the short amount of time with us, he has sprouted feathers like an adolescent human male sprouts body hair.

Haphazardly.

But it was undeniable. The bald spots on his head and throat were filling in and his wings seemed longer and fuller. Which helps explain how he managed to reach his perch about 6 feet higher than he had been.

He seemed quite happy with this new accomplishment and demonstrated his pleasure by squeezing out a watery bird turd which splattered on the floor, barely missing my bare feet and adding yet another clean up job for me.

Before getting a step stool to allow me to recapture him, I first went to our garage and retrieved the largest cat carrier we owned. I took some thin flat rope we had and strung it throughout the air holes of the cage and created a few swinging perches for him. I lined the bottom with newspaper and placed his basket inside. He wasn't happy about me taking him from the rod and even less about me placing him inside the carrier. I placed it on the coffee table with the front end facing the backyard so he'd have a bit of a view to enjoy. It wasn't a true cage but it would suffice until he was ready to go free.

Somehow I knew the easy part of this adventure was over.

Progress

The next couple of days were non-eventful. About 3am I would wake up, stumble into the kitchen and place a handful of dried cat food into a bowl and cover with water so it would be ready for his breakfast. Then back to bed. I rose every morning as the sun began to rise because HE woke up about that time and would begin chirping. If breakfast failed to roll in almost immediately, the cadence and volume would begin to increase until he was basically screaming with a machine gun rhythm which was sure to wake Grace up. Since I considered him to be MY project I wanted to prevent any inconveniences for her.

I'm pretty sure SHE felt the same way too…

Also not only was he growing feathers at an alarming rate but the color of his feathers were beginning to change. He was a black / brown color which I assumed made him a Mockingbird. But his feathers began to become brown. With a touch of a reddish tinge. I was no longer sure what I was raising.

Also I began slipping little bits of fruit to him. Slivers of apple, slices of grapes, cut up raisins were all gratefully accepted. But everything had to be fed to him. He refused to feed himself.

He Comes Out of the Closet

As previously stated he began to fill in his feathers and they started changing colors. He was an off shade of black/brown when we first found him. My first impressions were that he was either a Mockingbird or possibly a Blue Jay but later I wondered what I saw that hinted of a Blue Jay. No he had to be a Mockingbird but the feathers that came in were more a light shade of brown than black or grey. And in bright light there seemed to be a hint of red.

Definitely a mystery.

But all theories came tumbling down at one defining moment.

I had just fed him and was letting him play on the coffee table before I returned him to the cat carrier. Grace was sitting on the loveseat beside me. I held a sparkling earring that had belonged to my mother and he was enthralled with it. He snatched it from my fingers and was hopping around the table holding it in his beak. I pretended to try and take it away and he was expertly avoiding my attempts to remove it when our neighbors next door suddenly made a loud booming noise that frightened him. He leapt off of the table and made a clumsy landing on the floor. He quickly recovered and hopped frantically to safety under the coffee table. He looked right and left trying to determine where the danger may be.

And that's when it happened.

Suddenly a tuft of feathers on top of his head slowly raised up and we realized we were not looking at a Mockingbird but instead, a Northern Cardinal. Their most predominant features are the red coloring of the male and their crest of feathers on top of their heads which both sexes possess. They raise their crest of feathers for a number of reasons including being alarmed or scared.

Now this triggered a debate that persisted for months. What was his correct gender? Many people quickly pointed out that his feathers were the dull brown of female Cardinals even though I repeatedly informed them that I had learned it can take up to a year for males to turn the bright red normally associated with Cardinals and it was too soon to change his name from ROSCOE to ROSCOELINA. He, of course, didn't care.

It kind of reminded me of the time when our son, Chad, was just a tiny baby and so many people would come up and admire him, saying, "He looks just like his MOTHER!"

I always replied, "NOT WITH HIS PANTS OFF, HE DOESN'T!" I never got tired of saying it although I believe Grace quickly got tired of hearing it. But it always brought that line of conversation to a screeching halt!

Soon Roscoe was beginning to develop a sense of identity and independence. He still took food from my fingers but also he began to feed himself more consistently. When he was really hungry I was an acceptable servant to bring him morsels, tidbits or snacks. But once he began to fill up, even a bit he suddenly wanted nothing from the vileness of my fingers nor the filth of my palm. Instead he would eat from a shallow bowl or better yet, food spread across the coffee table top. Unfortunately he also had no compunction of throwing seeds to and fro in order to select one from the middle of the pile. The fact was that the one seed he desired was exactly like the others that he tossed away (mainly on the floor). After all, HE didn't have to clean up after himself. No, I did.

The servant boy. The lackey. The peon.

And his feathers continued to come in red.

Cleanliness is Next to Godliness

As previously stated, my clumsy efforts to feed him left him covered from top to bottom with caked on dried cat food. I don't know how he felt about it but I cringed whenever I looked at him and I would take a moistened paper towel and scrub him down a bit whenever he would let me. Sometimes he would struggle to get away from me and other times he would let me clean his beak, legs and feathers and he seemed to relish the way it made him feel. He would generally fluff up his feathers and flap his wings while chirping loudly with what assuredly was sheer joy.

I was on the lookout for a shallow bowl that he might want to bathe in and Grace produced one that I thought was too small. But I put it out for him anyway until I could find one a bit larger. But when I did find one that I thought would be perfect, he wouldn't use it but instead used the first one only.

I don't know if this is typical but this bird LOVED his baths. In colder weather I brought him his bowl filled with warm water. In the heat of summer, I placed ice chips in it. Spoiled bird.

Every day, around 9:30am, the show would begin. He would hop over to the small bowl and would do a "cannonball" into the pool. The first few seconds he merely stood in the water. Maybe he was adjusting to the water temperature but I believe he was simply relaxing and enjoying the sensation of the water on his feathers and skin.

And then he would begin…

First he would dip his head into the water, raise his head towards the sky and shake his head back and forth vigorously to release the droplets. Then he would move back and forth in the water while vigorously flapping his wings in and out of the water which splashed the water onto his back and tail (and virtually anything within a 3 foot radius!). Once he was soaked, he shook his wings and then his tail feathers. First slowly then with blinding speed and then he would stop and savor the moment before doing it over again and again. The water flew in all directions. Once I was sitting on the loveseat and he was bathing inside of his cage. I was sitting at least 6 feet away and was getting very wet from his ministrations. Several times I videoed him in slow motion and it was fascinating to watch. His body undulated from front to back but most interesting was the camera picked up the sounds his wet wings produced. There was a repeated "WHOOMP! WHOOMP! **WHOOOOOMP**!" coming from his wet wings. I was never tired of watching and listening to it.

Sometimes he would be finished in 30 or so seconds and other times it continued for up to 5 minutes. Often the bowl would be nearly emptied when he finished, while the nearby windows, the floor and myself required cleaning and drying.

While he was young this spectacle took place on the coffee table and when he was older it happened in his cage. On the coffee table he would hop out of the bowl and then hop around the table while flapping his wings to dry off. If the sun was shining he would hop to the sunspot on the table and enjoy the sun's warmth. In his cage he would hop up and down on the network of perches before moving to the open doors of the cage and then flying around the room several times. He would either land on one of the decorations in the room and sit while enjoying the sensation or he would return to his cage where he would either sit on one of the perches I had set up on top of the cage or go inside and move up and down the network of perches until he found the one that made him happy at that moment. After a short relaxation he invariably went to the "buffet" at the bottom of his cage to capture a cricket or worm for a snack.

Spoiled bird…

Other Stories

Our life was not solely birds. Our little piece of Paradise, or as my buddy, Ben, called it: "THE ESTATE", had plenty of other bits of wildlife to entertain us. Like the day after Hurricane Irma sent a tornado to our neighbor Charlie at 5am to rip off his big screened room and dump it in our front yard, knocking down 9 of his oak trees and 4 of ours. We were trapped for 2 days. We almost bought that house too, strictly for the screened in room. Little did we know we would ultimately get it for FREE. Sadly it wasn't of much value to us in that condition.

Then after the storm passed, Grace watched one of our cats marching across the backyard where it drops off into the creek. Soon a second followed the first and then the third came after the other two. Then she saw a fourth cat which she recognized as Bigfoot, keeping lockstep with the first three. Only then did she notice the first 3 had short stubby little tails. Bobcats, returning to wherever their lair was and our cat was making sure they left us. Or maybe he was hoping to join their club.

We had a plethora of raccoons and possums that boldly came up to our home. When we first bought the place, I would fish on the dock after the sun went down. Eventually I'd hear the sound of toenails coming down the steps and it would be a young 'coon. He'd retreat back up the steps away from me but I'd pop the head off of a bait shrimp and toss it over my shoulder. He would stop and come back and soon I would hear the crunching as he would chew it up and swallow. I'd send another, but closer to me and soon he would be walking around my feet or would hop up on the bench next to me, waiting for another morsel.

ONE TIME and only one time, I fed him from my hand. I only did it for bragging rights and never did it again. Raccoon can carry rabies and though it was highly unlikely one this young would be infected but why tempt fate?

I'd already had MY rabies shots! And did not wish to repeat the experience.

When I was 4 years old we had a little Rat Terrier. One night we had family over for a visit and when it was my bedtime I went around and kissed everybody goodnight. Then I got down on the floor where our little dog was curled up asleep and I gave him a kiss too. Right on his forehead. What a stupid move.

The poor doggie came out of a sound sleep and frightened by the unexpected act of affection, immediately went on the offensive. Needle sharp teeth put a double row of bite marks on MY forehead! Realizing he had done something bad, he slinked away and hid. While the bites really didn't hurt much, I suddenly had a small flash flood of blood running down my face. My mother grabbed me up and soon I was in the bathroom getting a heavy application of either iodine or mercurochrome all over my forehead.

Now THAT hurt!

The next day I was taken to our pediatrician who decided that even though our dog had had his rabies shot, a bite this close to the brain required immediate preventative care in the form of a series of 12 rabies shots. Back then the mere mention of rabies sent a chill through one's veins and anybody exposed to the virus received a daily shot. But these were no ordinary injections given to the arm or buttocks, no these were given into the belly and the needle was around 8 inches long.

I was a typical kid when it came to shots. They were to be avoided at all costs. My brother once was bitten by a nonvenomous rat snake (he had been chasing some smaller children with it when the poor snake became frightened and being held loosely decided to steady himself by latching onto Mike's hand between the thumb and forefinger.) The snake had such a grip that it required prying its mouth open with a screwdriver to free my sibling. When told he would receive a tetanus shot he began crying and begged my mother to tell the doctors he had been bitten by a turtle. Somehow I guess he believed that would prevent his shot. It didn't work.

Anyway I received an immediate rabies shot and every morning for the next 11 days, I was taken to the doctor for another. But for some reason I refused to cry and this upset the nurses and the doctor. One nurse told my mother when she first saw the massive needle she became nauseous and when I wouldn't cry even the doctor begged me to let out a scream or do something. But instead with my eyes screwed shut I endured this act of barbarism. Even today, I can not watch a needle being inserted into my body nor even watch one on tv or a movie.

I'd make a lousy junkie.

Now when we ended up with pet chickens, all of my beloved raccoons became my mortal enemies. Raccoons love to eat chicken and I soon tired of finding a pile of feathers instead of one of my favorite hens. And so I bought a few live traps and started catching these bandits of the night and taking them to a swamp about 10 miles away, far from anybody's home.

Okay, I shouldn't admit this next part.

There is a Florida law called the Varmint Law which requires any trapped animal which is not considered to be endangered must either be released on the spot or destroyed. It was to prevent people from catching a problem animal and releasing it where it becomes somebody else's problem. No doubt a good law at a different time and in a different environment when people typically lived off of the land. But that is not the situation today in my community. But it's the law and once I learned about it, I stopped my capture and relocate project..

While I was still doing it, I drove my prisoners far away to a secluded boat ramp next to a swamp and released them. They couldn't harm anybody and were back in a natural state conducive to their survival. I thought it was a win-win for everybody, especially the 'coon since it didn't get a bullet in the head.

The Story of Coondini

This is a true story and took place before I learned I was an environmental criminal.

We have a long driveway and it ends between our house and garage. A friend offered me some pieces of palm tree trunks when he cut down some of his palms. I lined them up along the end of the driveway and mounted reflectors on them so if anybody came to visit us after dark, this would hopefully prevent them from driving through our privacy fence and into our neighbor's living room. And the area behind this wall of palms was a great place for me to spread our chickens' feed each morning. It kept everything neat and tidy and they went there throughout the day when they needed a snack. Unfortunately they rarely finished it all and the birds, squirrels and raccoons knew it was a source for a quick meal.

One evening right before nightfall, Grace and I came home. As we pulled up to the house we noticed a young raccoon eating some of the chicken feed I had put out for the kids earlier that day. He immediately ran away. I got out of the car and went to escort any feathered stragglers to the coop and close it up for the night. As I returned to the house I saw our little visitor had returned. Again he scurried away but I knew he would soon be back.

So I baited up a trap and set it out. The traps I use are "live capture" traps. A door with 2 strong springs is raised up and held open by a small piece of wire. Further back in the trap is a raised piece of metal that serves as a trigger. Even further into the trap bait is placed. I have learned to wire small cans to the back end of the trap and partially fill it with something smelly like fish based wet cat food or bacon grease. The can is wired about halfway up that back wall and partially covered with the can lid or some other object that will prevent the raccoon (or possum) from reaching in through the wire of the trap and snatching a morsel. You want to convince them to enter the trap and move towards the bait. Hopefully they will set the trigger off and ths spring launched front door will slam shut capturing your little visitor. This is much more complicated than I just described because on numerous occasions I have found the bait gone and the trap door wide open. More confusing is finding the bait gone, the trap door down and no critter inside. I mean I have to use both hands setting the traps and it's a challenge to open the door because it is a very strong spring.

That evening I placed the baited trap behind the wall of palm stumps with the back of the trap firmly up against one, among the uneaten chicken feed and then walked into the house.

About 20 minutes later I stepped out on the porch in time to see our little masked marauder slip behind the row of stumps and making a beeline for the trap. I listened intently to hear the sound of the trapdoor slam shut meaning he was caught. But I heard nothing and I knew he was trying to steal the bait through the trap's bars. Many animals will resist entering a trap and will first try a little burglary, especially raccoons. Instinctively they sense a danger and try theft but hunger will then drive them to enter.

I decided to have a little fun with him. Silently I sneaked down and was soon standing directly over him on the opposite side of the tree sections. He had one forepaw deep between the bars of the trap trying to snag the bait. He looked exactly like a small child with his hand in a cookie jar. He was concentrating so hard on a free meal he was not aware of my presence.

My first thought was to bop him on top of his head with my finger but I quickly dismissed that idea. The top of a raccoon's head is very close to its teeth and while this one looked quite healthy, raccoons are susceptible to rabies. And as I described earlier, as a very young boy, a miscalculation with our pet dog resulted in me enduring a 12 day course of anti-rabies shots, an experience I'd prefer to avoid.

So instead of touching the small 'coon, I quietly asked, "What are YOU doing?" Startled, he stopped his efforts, withdrew his paw and looked up at me but did not bolt. Instead he did the strangest thing. He stood up on his hind legs and studied me. No fear, just as bold as he could be.

I immediately froze in position. I wanted to see what he would do and didn't want to scare him away.

Then he dropped down on all fours and slowly strolled around the trap to the far side of it. Again, he stopped and stood on his hind legs and peered at me for about 5 seconds, then he dropped to all 4 legs but this time slowly walked around the trap again TOWARDS ME to his original spot and then again stood up, to check me out some more. There was NO fear in him. Just curiosity.

I was beginning to wish I had a video camera recording what was happening. I knew nobody would believe what I was seeing. Little did I know that what was coming would be even more surprising.

Three times he traveled around the trap each time standing up for a closer look at me. I continued to act like a statue to avoid spooking him. .

As he was again approaching where I stood, one of our cats, Bigfoot, walked up and stood beside my left leg. I was trying to figure out how to chase the cat away without moving. I was certain his presence would chase the raccoon away and I was still enjoying watching his antics. The raccoon returned to his original place below me. The cat and the coon were on opposite sides of the same piece of palm trunk and it was as if their next move was choreographed and rehearsed. At the same time, they BOTH stood up on their rear legs and they looked at each other. Maybe 6 inches separated them but there was no surprise, anger or fright between them. No snarling, hissing or baring of teeth, it was like 2 old friends meeting in a bar. They stared at each other for a few seconds then simultaneously leaned in and touched noses!! I was so shocked. It was so cute and unexpected. Now I was REALLY wishing this was videotaped. It would have easily won the $100,000 prize on AMERICA'S FAVORITE VIDEOS! The raccoon dropped down on all four paws and slowly walked away. Then I watched him enter the trap and it slammed shut.

I had him.

I went inside and advised Grace he was trapped. She had just watched the weather forecast and since it was supposed to storm all night, she suggested we go release him now. I agreed.

I went outside and spread newspaper in the back of Grace's Volvo XC60 and then picked up the trap and placed it on the paper. Now this is when most trapped animals get very upset and start trying to escape. They will usually walk around the trap once or twice looking for a way out. Then they will either try to hide by curling up with their noses tucked in a corner with their tails wrapped across their eyes. It's the classical IF I CAN'T SEE YOU, YOU CAN'T SEE ME move. Or they try to be a badass by backing into a corner and planting their front paws firmly down. They will glare at you daring you to try anything. They may bare their teeth, growl or snarl. But not this one. Instead he calmly stood in the center of the trap and continued to study me! I stood there talking softly to him to keep him calm. I was saying silly things like "Don't worry. We're going to take you to a great place with lots of food and hot female raccoons. He watched me and seemed to be understanding me as I prattled on. After about 15 or 20 seconds he extended one of his forelegs through the bars and offered me its paw. The paw was held palm up and not knowing the proper raccoon etiquette, I placed my forefinger in its palm and it gently wrapped its paw around my finger. In return I wrapped the rest of my fingers around his paw.

We were bonding! We were becoming buddies!

Grace came out and started the car and I lowered the trunk lid and got in the passenger seat. In the back we could hear him munching down on the bacon grease bait. It sounded like he was enjoying it a great deal.

After we had traveled about a mile we heard the trap rattle hard for about 2 seconds, then it became silent. Ten seconds later, Grace made the comment that it seemed like he was getting closer. I told her to not be silly because I have to use both hands to open those traps. The door has 2 very strong springs and it's not easy to open and set. Certainly he would not be able to open it from the inside and step through to freedom without it noisily slamming shut.

I was VERY certain of that. It was definitely impossible.

Then I felt it.

Something fuzzy lightly brushed my right ear.

I looked over my shoulder and saw a wet nose and two black shining eyes only a few inches away from my face! My new friend was perched on the headrest of my seat!!!! Mere inches away! It was his whiskers that tickled my ear.

After careful consideration I realize I may have overreacted a bit. All my life I was known as the guy who did not panic. I always stayed cool and collected. And I blew it in that instant! I think if I had not reacted, we would have continued on our trip and he would have ridden along with us with no problems. Instead I said, no I screamed, something unrepeatable and Grace wisely asked no questions nor delayed her actions. Instead she immediately stepped on the brakes, slowing the car and pulled halfway onto the shoulder of the road. She then released her seatbelt, unlocked the door, opened the driver's door and lithely stepped out with the car still slowly rolling forward. And for reasons I still do not understand, she turned the headlights off. Since there are no streetlights on this stretch of road, I could not see what was ahead of the car.

LEAVING ME BEHIND! So much for that "Till Death do we part" crap in our wedding vows. Maybe there is a raccoon clause I did not read.

I started to follow her lead and also abandon ship but I quickly quelled my panic. I realized the car was still moving forward and would eventually roll into the deep ditch on the side of the road or flatten a neighbor's mailbox or smack into something that would both cause damage to somebody's property and bang up our vehicle. I had a mental image of me trying to explain to our insurance agent how I was in a driverless vehicle with a wild raccoon in our car, practically in my lap and why my policy should cover whatever damage was done . He's a great guy but I'm uncertain how much of a sense of humor he may have. So I quickly unbuckled my seatbelt and grabbed the steering wheel with my left hand. I have short stubby legs but even so normally I can't cross my legs in the front seat of this car, yet I somehow managed to throw my left leg over the console, which is about 4 inches higher than the seats, AND THE GEAR SHIFTER of the vehicle (without emasculating myself!), which is at least another 6 inches high, and lifted myself up with my right leg until my left foot made contact with the brake pedal. I stomped on the brake until the car completely stopped and then put the car in PARK. Next I clumsily pulled my leg back over the console and exited out of the passenger door, which I also left open so our furry little passenger could easily follow me out into the open world.

The whole time the raccoon remained calmly on the top of my headrest but once I skipped out we watched as he jumped into my now empty seat and then trampolined up onto the dashboard. He enjoyed the view for a second or two, then leapt into the driver's seat but did not hop through the open doorway. Instead he paused and stood up on his hind legs and grasped the steering wheel with his front paws and stared out of the windshield, as if he was driving the now stopped car. He was looking much like a small child pretending to be driving his parents' car. I have always wondered if he was making "**VROOM! VROOM! VROOM!**" car engine sounds in his mind as he pretended to drive, much like I used to do.

In 1988 and 1989, Saturday Night Live, the live comedy show, had a series of skits featuring "TOONCES, THE DRIVING CAT" in which a puppet cat named Toonces, drove its owners around in their car as they sat in the backseat. All the skits ended with the car and its occupants going off of a tall cliff. This looked exactly like one of those skits except we had a live raccoon. And no cliff.

After a few seconds he jumped out of the open door and ran into the dark and probably back to our house. I'm sure he got there before we did.

Well we looked at each other in total amazement and then we started laughing uncontrollably and basically laughed about it until the next afternoon. Because I still can't figure out how he managed to escape from that trap, we named him "HAIRY COONDINI" after Harry Houdini, the legendary escape artist of the 1920S.

Years later, Iam still wondering how he escaped from the trap so quietly and we still laugh over it.

Lord, I wish I had a video of the whole episode!

Grace is <u>NOT</u> Happy!

For some reason I have had a green thumb and been able to successfully grow plants. Back in the 1970s, macrame became a popular pastime and especially hangers for potted plants. A friend gave me a hanger he macramed himself and it held a small potted Jade plant. I accepted it with good (I hope) graces but inside I sneered at it, especially the plant. I had no expectations of it surviving under my care but amazingly it not only survived but thrived becoming a real showcase with large thick trunks and symmetrical limbs covered with thick green leaves. I learned to prune it to shape it into the forms I wanted. Before long I was raising a number of plants and became a member of various horticultural societies devoted to begonias, ferns, succulents and roses. I also became a very active member of the Men's Garden Club of Jacksonville. We had a member, Jim Watson, who was a retired Agricultural Agent for the County. EVERYBODY knew Jim. He was a true Southern gentleman and looked like everybody's grandfather. He was quite a character with a quick wit and an extensive knowledge of most plants and how to raise them. He had a weekly newspaper column and a weekly tv show on the Public Broadcasting channel. I enjoyed his show but I had no idea how popular it was. But I was about to learn.

At every house we've owned, one of my first projects was to build a greenhouse. At our monthly meetings of The Men's Garden Club we were encouraged to bring plants to show. I had a reputation for growing beautiful, healthy but unusual plants and my exhibits were generally well received. Jim especially enjoyed my participation and often came up after the meetings to compliment me, ask questions and share information.

One evening I received a call at home from Jim. He informed me that he and a cameraman would be dropping by in 2 days so he could film his next show in MY greenhouse! Basically I had a day to prepare.

The next day was a flurry of preparation. I repotted plants or scrubbed pots to clean them up. I pruned and watered and brought in huge bags of cypress mulch to cover the dirt floor in several inches of new, clean and fragrant mulch. Then I had to rearrange every plant at least 3 times to showcase my best looking specimens. These were displayed at the front of the shelves that held my chlorophyll laden babies. The ones that were barely alive were placed at the back where they were barely visible at all.

I had made the Big Time! At least in the horticulture group. (I once saw a gardening apron for keeping your clothes clean. It carried the message,

YOU CAN LEAD A HORTICULTURE, BUT YOU CAN'T MAKE HER THINK! Genius!)

Well Jim and Don Agnew, his producer and cameraman arrived. I knew Don because I worked with his wife. Now Jim had an old folksy Deep South way of talking and often he would ramble on one point or another which could occasionally be hard to follow and sometimes he would pause and suddenly you realized he had asked a question but you weren't sure what he had asked. It was endearing to his viewers but not so much for his guests. A couple of times he did this to me but happily I had followed enough of his monolog to respond with answers that sort of made sense.

But often he would break protocol and ignore the beautiful plants I had placed in the foreground and would reach over to the back plants that were put there because they lacked that star quality I wanted to give. Nope, he would pull out a ragged, half dead plant that was only days away from the compost pile and hold it in front of the camera, which Don would dutifully zoom in on which served to emphasize its many flaws, while Jim would say, "So tell us about THIS beautiful plant you have here!"

I wanted to strangle him on live tv.

Except this wasn't live, it was being filmed so Don could edit it.

Well several days later I learned Don had an evil streak. He came up to the office to see Pat, his wife, and upon seeing me he rushed over and shook my hand thanking me for "a most entertaining show". Then with a totally evil smile, he informed me that Jim had made an awkward statement that went over Jim's head, my head and even his own, until he was editing the tape. In fact he said because of the speech mannerisms Jim used, it was only when his assistant pointed this out did he realize the significance of the statement.

He said he deliberated long about removing the statement and even ran it past his bosses, but since he knew I'd be a good sport about it, he left it in. He thought Jim's viewers would appreciate a good laugh. When I pressed him for details, he said I'd have to wait and see it when the rest of Jacksonville saw it too.

I advised him I had a good lawyer and he laughed and said he'd risk it.

And so, Monday evening at 7pm, I slipped a blank VHS tape into the VCR and hit record as the show began. The show always began and ended live at the studio. Jim would discourse live on the weather, various upcoming events, and local stories or gossip before launching the pre-recorded segments. But soon enough, there I was standing beside Jim in my sizable greenhouse. I was rather impressed by how the sweat bands at my armpits glistened in the lights from the camera. Jim started by discussing the layout and construction of my greenhouse and was very complimentary of it when I heard Grace giggling and then laughing. At what, I was curious.

"Oh you missed it," she said. "Wait until it's over and we'll rewind it."

Suddenly our telephone started ringing. I tried to ignore it but when it stopped ringing, in only a second or two it started up again. After several cycles like this I snatched the phone up. It was my good friend and poker adversary, Ben, and he was laughing so hard I couldn't understand what he was saying. After several failed attempts to regain control, he finally blurted out, "Well DOES she?'

"Do what?" I asked. This only set him off again into braying like a donkey with peals of laughter. I hung up.

The phone immediately started ringing again and I snatched it up, "Dammit, Ben! I'm trying to watch this. Leave me alone!" But I heard the quiet reserved voice of Joe, another poker buddy. Joe, a devoted church goer and a true gentleman, was chuckling. "Great show, buddy. Debby and I really enjoyed it. But Debby is wondering if we can borrow your greenhouse for a couple of hours?" "For what?" I blurted. Then he lost control and I heard him shout at his wife, "He doesn't know!" Then he started laughing like I'd never heard him do before. I hung up again.

The phone again started ringing. I let it go.

Finally, it was over. Wordlessly, Grace hit the rewind button and we again watched Jim start the show. Finally Grace whispered I needed to pay attention. Seconds later, I heard it.

My good friend, Jim Watson, who probably never had a dirty thought in his life, asked the innocent question, "Does your wife ever come out and fool around in the greenhouse with you?" Me, who has had PLENTY of dirty thoughts, missed the implication and replied, "Well not lately…"

I felt my face grow red with embarrassment. Then I also lost control and started laughing. The next day and the two after I had a lot of comments from friends and coworkers, then it died off. However they repeat the shows Saturday mornings and then a slightly lessened reaction picked back up.

But whenever Jim took vacation or as his health started giving him problems and prevented him from doing a regular show, they repeated past shows and this was obviously a favorite because two or three times a year for several years, someone would tell me, "I saw you on tv last night…"

But my successes with plants did not carry over to Grace. And for the most she didn't care. She was happy to let me handle the greenery in our lives.

With two exceptions…

Our first home was a delightful little bungalow in the Avondale area of Jacksonville. When Jacksonville burned to the ground in 1901, Riverside and Avondale were two of the areas that were first rebuilt. There are many huge glorious houses in the area including a number of riverfront mansions as well as beautiful large homes on more modest lots. One is made entirely of white marble, including the garage. Imposing and beautiful, I'm sure the marble helps keep it nice and cool in our sweltering summers.

Bet it's a bitch to heat though.

And there are MUCH smaller houses in the area that are still a joy to behold. Grace's grandmother helped me buy one of these four months before our wedding. Two bedrooms, one bath and a fireplace that smoked constantly but it had a wonderful wrap-around front porch and a large corner lot and so much charm that everybody loved it. When we moved into a larger house, 7 years later, we used it for rental and it was never empty for more than 24 hours. After 25 years of rental income we sold it to help us buy our Yulee place and it had immediate buyers. We blew our realtor's mind when we got every penny of our "ridiculous" asking price. The woman who bought it had been keeping an eye on it for two years, hoping it would go on the market. Two years later she sold it for double what she paid.

We built our first greenhouse there and I spent untold hours pottering around in it and among the many bushes and trees I planted in the yard were three Anna apple trees.

It is simply too hot in Florida to grow apples but Anna apples were supposed to tolerate the heat and bear fruit in Florida. Well every spring they would be loaded with blossoms which excited Grace very much and she would baby those trees trying to encourage actual fruit from them.

Not a chance.

Every year the blossoms would bravely try and hold on but one by one they would fall to the ground.

Except for one year.

One year, one blossom hung in there. And soon a small round ball of future apple sweetness formed. Grace marveled at it and watched it grow and develop into an actual apple. She watered and fertilized the tree and pulled the weeds that dared to enter its domain. She shooed away any squirrels or birds that even looked at it. And Barney could not pee on it either.

I suppose I should introduce Barney. Barney was our very large yellow Labrador Retriever. Barney was all heart, tail and tongue. Just as sweet as could be, he loved everybody and everybody loved him. I kept finding bits of aluminum foil in the yard and one day noticed our back neighbor dropping something in the yard. An extremely dedicated vegetarian, she was cooking a roast every week for our dog!!! And she'd wrap it in foil to keep the dirt off of it. I told her to simply drop it as a bit of dirt wouldn't hurt him but I wondered how the foil he doubtlessly swallowed would affect him.

There were numerous people in the area who didn't know OUR name but all knew Barney based on the greetings I heard him receive from passersby all day. Especially amusing was a young boy who tried to teach Barney to roll over while demonstrating the proper technique by rolling around on the ground. He was not successful, but I'm sure his parents wondered why he kept coming home so dirty.

Now while Barney would not roll over on command, one talent he had was he could EAT! Almost anything. We only learned of 3 things he would not gulp down: strawberries, pistachio pudding and Pantry Pride Dog Food. Anything else was palatable to him. Anything.

I had a huge planter of small barrel cacti on the front porch. The size of baseballs with large hard razor sharp thorns, I was surprised to learn someone was apparently stealing them. But they were stealing them one at a time. Very strange.

One day I saw Barney chewing on something but he was chewing slowly and carefully. Curious I pried his massive jaws open and reached in to retrieve his morsel. With a loud yelp I pulled my hand back full of cacti spines. The dumb dog was eating my succulents. After I spent several painful minutes removing the saliva coated thorns before lugging the planter to the greenhouse where it was locked up. To this day I can not comprehend how he was able to eat them.

And so finally Grace made one of her daily inspections of the apple tree and determined it was time to "harvest the crop". Now most people would have simply plucked the fruit from the tree, but not my wife. Nope. An event this momentous required a certain decorum, a particular protocol. And so she went inside and found the perfect basket from her large collection. Then a cloth napkin had to be folded, just so, and placed in the basket. Then a pair of gardening gloves and some garden shears. Once she was properly equipped, she marched to the tree only to see THE TREE WAS EMPTY!!! NO APPLE!!! Frantically she searched the tree again then the ground beneath it. Then she noticed Barney! He was standing about 20 feet away and had something in his mouth! Without hesitation she leapt on his broad back and wrestled him to the ground in a way that would have made any rodeo rider proud. Possessing a strength I did not know she had, she pried his massive jaws apart and triumphantly pulled her soggy, slightly chewed prize from his mouth and held it aloft.

She stormed into our kitchen where she washed The Forbidden Fruit for about 20 minutes. Then in the manner of The Original Eve in the Garden of Eden, she offered me half. Generously I refused, insisting it was all hers. And so it was and she proudly ate the entire thing.

I didn't kiss her for 3 days…

Now Grace loves African Violets and there are 2 critical components to success in growing and blooming African Violets. That's water and light.

Water is no problem as we are on a well and we have fantastic water. For one thing the water is apparently naturally soft water, meaning it doesn't have the dissolved minerals that cause water spots, pipe damage, bad taste or pipe damage. I once sold water conditioning equipment and as far as I know there is not supposed to be naturally soft water in Florida. One of the major sources for the dissolved minerals is limestone and Florida is basically a huge chunk of limestone. Yet we get no water spots, no bad taste or smell and if we leave the dishpan full of water we will still have suds and bubbles up to 3 days later. Amazing.

As far as light went, our humble little palace boasts unbelievable amounts of natural sunlight. Every room has large unobstructed windows but the sunroom offers the best. And it was in this room that Grace's thumb took on a greenish hue as her green thumb started to "blossom". Her African Violets grew to disportionate sizes as even the dwarf varieties I loved to buy for her exploded with leaves dappled in white, yellow and cream. And the blooms looked like tiny fireworks with various shades and hues of purple, violet, pinks, white, red and a rare variety that bloomed a lime green.

She was proud of them and I was proud of her. I knew how much work she put into her "babies".

At least once a week she would take a solution of fertilizer infused water into the sunroom and she carefully pruned off dead or damaged flowers or leaves. She wiped the leaves clean of dust or cat hair. She topped off their water reservoirs and then gave each pot a quarter turn to keep the plants growing symmetrically.

Normally I sat in the sunroom whenever Roscoe was out of the cat carrier. I watched to make sure he didn't get into any trouble and I would bring him out and feed him. At first I continued with the cat food and fed him with my fingers and gradually introduced him to small pieces of fruit such as apples, blueberries or blackberries. He made it very evident he did not enjoy strawberries. I also gave him slivers of lettuce, cabbage, carrots and peas. I also slipped in small amounts of crushed peanuts or pecans. After hand feeding him a bit, I began placing his food on the table so he could become accustomed to feeding from the ground.

He enjoyed his greens very much and unfortunately I turned a blind eye to something that should have been evident.

Roscoe frequently landed on Grace's African Violets and I always shooed him away thinking he would stomp the fragile blooms and leaves.

Well once I was called away to take care of something and I decided to leave him outside of the carrier so he could get some exercise flying around. After all, what harm could he possibly do?

Well I was gone for about a half hour when I heard Grace shouting, "OH NO! OH NO!". Fearing the worst I ran into the room to see her standing over Roscoe and peering down on him with a distinct look of anger and distaste on her face. It was then that I realized he was perched in the midst of her prized African Violets and he was merrily plucking the fragile violets into pieces. Parts of leaves, stems and flowers were spread everywhere and he was obviously having the time of his life. As I watched he plucked a fat bloom from a plant and then proceeded to devour it with what was obvious joy.

Eating flowers? I had never considered them as a food source but apparently they were. And since they are the source of seeds, well it made more sense.

I plucked him off of his green perch and stuffed him back into the cat carrier. Then I went out of the room to face the music with my wife.

But I started thinking about what it might mean for him to be eating the flowers. Perhaps I was missing a whole source of nutrition for him. So the next morning after his "morning meal" and his daily bath, I stuffed him, protesting loudly, back into the carrier. Then I went out into the yard and picked a "salad" for him. First I gathered some green blades of grass, then I picked several flowers from various plants. I had planted many various plants with the idea of always having several plants in bloom year 'round. I tried to get various colors too. I washed them in the kitchen sink and placed them on a paper towel and placed them on the coffee table and then I opened the cat carrier and released the prisoner.

Normally he would take off and fly around the room a bit to stretch his wings but this time he made a beeline for his "salad bar" and literally dove into them. I was reminded of a kid on Christmas morning. He threw them around the table while sampling the various offerings and soon he was nibbling a few and others he broke off pieces and consumed them. I began to feel better about his impending release. If he stayed nearby I should have enough growing in the yard to keep him from starving to death. But I also needed to introduce him to live foods. Insects and worms.

A Game of Cricket

No, I'm not referring to the game enjoyed by the British population involving bats, balls and wickets. Whatever a wicket is. This was about the insect Gryllinae, the chirping insect that sings during the summer nights.

Disney fans refer to them as Jiminy.

I needed insects that Roscoe would easily find in the wild and would be likely to consume. Grasshoppers immediately came to mind but after several hours trying to find and capture some I had exactly: none. So I made a visit to the pet store to see what they had available and found they sell crickets. Crickets are fed to various creatures such as reptiles, fish and birds.

They are also a bit pricey at $.15 to $.25 each. After spending a fair amount of money on them, over a period of several months, I eventually remembered they are sold at bait and tackle stores at the modest price of $.02 each.

So I took a couple dozen back and introduced Roscoe to them. I would place a small one on the floor and he would soon be checking them out. But the first ones were smart enough to freeze and he would examine them but not move aggressively. But as soon as his back was turned they would turn on the afterburners and quickly scoot away. I would have to snatch them up and drop them in front of my feathered child and again they froze and he would lose interest. More than a couple managed to make a successful run for the border and would find sanctuary under the loveseat or the recliner and they would live in peace among the dust bunnies, indigenous to those locations. One went exploring further and one night my darling wife awoke at 2am to find one of them perched on the tip of her very cute nose. I am so proud to report that she neither screamed nor reacted in any way beyond sleepily capturing the adventurous insect and rising to toss the hapless creature into Roscoe's cage. Life with me has made this woman into a force to be reckoned with!

Another one, much luckier, made a journey the length of our house to live happily under our refrigerator for 10 days. At night it sang its little six legged heart out. It was quite soothing. Finally on the eleventh night a 2am journey to the bathroom allowed me to spot him out in the hallway and I swooped down and scooped him up. But my respect and admiration for its accomplishments would not allow me to return it to Roscoe's room and instead I set him free in the hydrangea outside by our porch.

But occasionally a cricket would make the mistake of breaking cover when Roscoe was watching and he would descend upon them and grab them in his beak. What happened next was not a pretty scene as he would then pull them apart and consume them although the rear legs were often left untouched.

Preparing for the End

I was working towards releasing my little friend and as he developed and grew, he also became an important part of my life and my affection for him grew as well. I was trying to expose him to different foods. In addition to the crickets, which were well received, I introduced him to dragon worms, which he would eat but they were definitely not a favorite of his.

But a real surprise came when I introduced him to earthworms.

THE EARLY BIRD GETS THE WORM. Who hasn't heard that statement? And as a child I saw cartoons in which birds of different species were all trying to catch and eat big fat juicy earthworms. They seemed to be the ultimate birdie meal.

And earthworms are common. I do a lot of composting and mulching and my soil is full of earthworms. After a heavy rain, I occasionally find earthworms laboriously crawling across my driveway after being washed out of the soil. I generally pick them up and toss them back into my compost piles before something makes a quick snack out of them.

And so I swung by the local bait store and got a container of earthworms to introduce him to this food option.

But he wouldn't eat them!

I was shocked when he seemed to stick his nose/beak in the air when I dangled one in front of him. I was floored by this reaction. Surely this was a mistake. But no, he wanted nothing to do with them. I tried force feeding them to him. I decided once one slithered down his throat, the dam would break and he would go nuts over them like all those cartoon birds. I would break them into pieces and shove them into his beak and he would promptly spit them out.

I refused to give up and he refused to cooperate. But after a number of failures, I released the rest into my garden and wished them well.

I don't remember who told me about wax worms but these became Cardinal Candy. These soft white grubs are found in the wax that forms honeycombs, which is where the name originated. They were actually pupae of a beetle and were a pest to beekeepers. I ordered them from eBay and would pay $23 to $25 for 500. He would scarf those like crazy. Since he wouldn't find them in our area I hesitated to give them to him. But I couldn't refuse him. He would generally eat 3 to 5 for breakfast.

And one time a moth somehow found its way into the sunroom. As it flew haphazardly around the room, Roscoe immediately took wing and attempted to capture it. I wish I had been able to video this event. The moth had some extraordinary moves and flew in patterns I would not have imagined a moth could do. It obviously knew it was in real danger and it zigged and zagged and flew up and down rapidly trying to get away. But as surprising as its movements were, so were Roscoe's. He literally followed every move that moth made. It reminded me of the dogfights in the movie TOP GUN which was about fighter pilots.

Finally Roscoe was able to knock it out of the air and the moth tumbled to the floor. As soon as it hit, Roscoe landed beside it and grabbed it in his beak. Again he dissected his poor victim before slowly eating the hapless insect with what appeared to be great joy.

Once before I watched a Mockingbird pursue a large Dragonfly for several minutes. I was amazed at the bird's determination as it also demonstrated some amazing mid-air gyrations while following it's prey until it eventually caught it's prey.

Well once I decided Roscoe knew what to eat, I made plans to release him. The weather forecast called for a few rainy days so I delayed his release until he would have good weather.

The night before the appointed date, I woke up at about 2:00am with a horrible realization. He knew WHAT to eat, but he didn't know WHERE to find his food. He was used to his meals being delivered by me. He would be expecting an old fat man to be feeding him!

I wasn't through with his training.

A Very Trying Morning!

The next morning I did not go and release him from the cat carrier and feed him as I normally did. Instead I went out into our garage, looking for a pan of some kind. I wanted one not too deep but with a bit of size to it and found the bottom to a cat litter box which fit the bill. Then I pulled up a couple of handfuls of grass and leaves and threw in a couple of twigs and small sticks.

I took this combination and placed it on the floor of the sunroom alongside the coffee table. I then placed a half dozen crickets and some mealworms into it and then took him out and placed him on the coffee table so he could see into the pan. I then sat on the floor behind the pan.

The idea was to prepare him for finding food on his own on the ground. This would be necessary for him to know where to look and what to look for. Now I'm certain he saw the menu in the pan but he did not want to serve himself. Instead he would fly to my head, shoulders, arms or my lap and expected me to provide his breakfast. When I refused to do so, he would get agitated and vocally expressed his displeasure. Often he would land on the floor beside me and hop back and forth while chirping loudly and often. He would become enraged at the poor service he was receiving and his hopping and indignant chirping reminded me of a tiny feathered Rumplestiltskin. Then he would hop on my legs or into my lap all while complaining loudly about how the service in the joint had fallen off and management better do something about it immediately. He could throw quite a temper tantrum.

Obviously I would NOT be receiving a tip for my efforts!

It soon became a true battle of the wills. Now I don't hold with astrology but if you do it might be worth mentioning that I am a Taurus, The Bull! A Taurus is renowned for being stubborn and I freely admit that I am. But I failed to recognize that based on his approximate age when we found him, HE WAS A TAURUS TOO! I don't know if astrology applies to non-humans as well but he would have made a good example to prove that it does. He was as stubborn as I was and he wanted his way.

I must admit, I nearly gave in to him several times. He was so cute throwing his feathered tantrums but mainly I knew he must be very hungry and it hurt me to deny him. But I also realized this was a truly necessary lesson that he had to learn and if I gave in it would only be harder the next time. After all, there is no room service in the wild.

Several times I picked him up and placed him in the pan with either a cricket or a worm in front of him but being in that container scared him and he would immediately fly out. And so I would then place him on the rim of the pan where he was merely a few inches away from his nourishment but again he would fly off.

My legs started to cramp and I had not had my breakfast either. I had decided I would not eat until he did. As my stomach growled in harmony with his, I again was tempted to take the easy way out and let him win and feed him. But pride kept me on track. I was damned if I was going to lose to a few ounces of feathers.

Two more hours passed.

Grace stuck her head in the room several times and asked if I wanted something to eat. I did but he still had not eaten and I decided I could hold out as long as he could. Besides, it would be poor sportsmanship to eat in front of him.

Well little birds require constant feedings and he was no exception. With all the fussing and cussing I was receiving it was obvious he was getting very hungry. Finally he flew to the rim of the pan and perched. A small cricket was laboriously climbing upward and was close to the lip of the pan. Callously I flicked him off as Roscoe was maneuvering towards a possible breakfast. I was treated to a VERY dirty look from my young protege as he realized the potential free meal had been removed. He gazed down into the pan and saw the worms and crickets crawling and hopping just a very few inches below him. He began working his way around the rim of the pan watching intently at the juicy morsels just below him. Each time a cricket would decide to "go over the top" by climbing the sides of the pan, I would wait until he was practically there and flick him off and back to the bottom of the pan. Each time Roscoe would have worked his way along the rim of the pan so he could personally "greet" the escapee as it went all the way to freedom. Of course Roscoe's plans for greeting the cricket was a free trip down the bird's gullet. And so, I would get a look of exasperation from the Feathered Freeloader and the distinct impression he would not forget that betrayal.

I could almost hear his stomach growling. I definitely could hear MINE. The two of us had missed breakfast and lunchtime was rapidly approaching.

Then he gave me a look that assured me the end of THIS trial was nearly here and with a look of resignation he hopped and dropped towards the floor of the pan. However just before landing he turned on the afterburners and with a furious beating of his wings he reversed direction and flew up and back to the rim of the pan.

RATS!!! So close.

Then in rapid succession he did this roundtrip 3 more times. A quick drop and an in air change of decision. People generally do not know that a Cardinal can hover, much like a Hummingbird. They don't have the ability to maneuver like a Hummingbird but they can definitely hang in one spot for several seconds.

 On the fourth attempt he allowed his feet to land in the bottom of the pan for about a half second before relaunching and then again. I was holding my breath while mentally cheering him on.

After all, I was hungry too!

And then he dropped again. He landed and was about to fly up again when he hesitated.

And he saw the cricket at his feet.

And he POUNCED!

He snatched that cricket and in about 2 seconds had swallowed it cleanly. Then he was looking around for seconds and quickly found a mealworm and soon the cricket had company in Roscoe's gullet.

Then he decided he had spent enough time here and flew up and circled the room a few times in what had to be a Victory Lap.

I was beaming and basking in the glow of a successful mission. In no time at all he landed back on the rim of the pan and almost immediately he dropped and continued to hunt.

I left the room, hobbling from cramped legs, a sore back and aching backside and went to eat a well deserved lunch.

During the next few days I started adding more grass, leaves and pine straw to the pan and adding fewer victims in order to make it harder for him to find food and to make him actually hunt for his meals. NO MORE FREEBIES!

While I revelled in his new found talent, it also made me sad because of what was soon to happen…

Free At Last!

The day I had been dreading was finally here. I had managed to stall a couple of days more due to rainy weather but I had run out of excuses. I fed him until he couldn't hold another wax worm and then I watched him fly around the room and play for another half hour before gently capturing him in my hands. I softly pressed his head to my cheek and gave him a little kiss on his head before placing him back in the cat carrier and Grace joined me as I carried him to our neighbor's yard. I had gotten permission to release him there for several reasons. One was that they have fewer trees and bushes and I wanted to be able to keep an eye on him for his initial period of time on his own. Another was that our cats were less likely to go over there. They are natural predators and had long had an interest in him. I wanted him to have every chance I could give him.

We had brought lawn chairs with us so we could more comfortably observe him so I set one up and placed the cat carrier in it and opened the door.

Immediately there was a reddish brown streak out and up! He flew up into the branches of a nearby tall pine tree. He perched on a limb and then traveled up the tree to a couple of higher limbs. It was like watching a small boy being set loose into a playground for the first time and trying out the Jungle Gym.

Then he flew to a second tree but only seconds later he zipped across the property into the next neighbor's yard and disappeared!

It took me a few seconds to realize he was gone. Really, really gone.

My heart began to sink. I thought I might enjoy watching him a bit longer. We waited a bit then folded our chairs and trudged through the gate back to our place.

But just as fast there was a flash of color into the bushes that line both sides of the fence. Now he was playing in the neighbor's shrubs, hopping up and down into the thick foliage. We would catch a glimpse of him for a few seconds and then he would plunge deeper into the foliage and vanish. I was desperately trying to video him and he made it a challenge as he dipped and dove and hopped and flew through the azaleas that thrive there. Then he popped up on the outer branches and gave us a "come hither" look and then again disappeared into the greenery.

We retreated further into our yard and set up our chairs near our blueberry thicket. He promptly followed us and went into the blueberries and again disappeared. They were far from ripe but he sampled a few and promptly dropped them from his beak. Realizing he was hungry I slipped away and went into our house and retrieved the container of waxworms from the refrigerator. When I returned Grace told me he was obviously looking for me. I saw him perching on the top of the thicket and I slowly approached him. As I did, he began to work his way down among the branches to my level and then came to the front of the bushes. I extended my hand with 2 fat waxworms. He ate them and then stayed there looking at me expectedly. I extended my hands slowly to him and he did not retreat. Gently I cupped him into my hands and carried him into the house and released him back into the sunroom. He drank greedily from his water bowl and when I placed the cat carrier on the coffee table he entered it voluntarily and promptly fell asleep. I closed the door to the carrier to the sound of gentle birdy snores. And a huge smile filled my face and tears of pure joy filled my eyes.

And at the same time I silently cursed myself for retrieving him and bringing him back inside. Should I have simply left him there to fend for himself? Was he really ready? Would he survive?

I left him alone most of the next day. The following morning I again stuffed him with as much as he could hold and again carried him outside but this time we stayed in our own yard as we locked the cats inside. I carried him to the middle of our yard and when I released him he flew across the yard and up to the tallest limb of our pecan tree. But as soon as he landed on the limb, a pair of Mockingbirds flew up and both smacked him off of the limb. He recovered in midair and returned to the limb and immediately a pair of Cardinals, a male and a female also attacked him viciously. He threw himself off of the limb and flew straight as an arrow back to me, chirping furiously the whole way. The message was clear: "Daddy! Daddy! Those bullies are being mean to me!" He landed on top of my head and I again captured him in my hands. He was trembling and shaking and I decided that was enough for today and I carried him inside.

I took him to the sunroom and started to release him but I had a premonition that I should look before I leap. And it was a good decision too. Lying in the corner of the room where he could not be easily seen was Sparky, our senior cat. I needed to go outside and retrieve the cat carrier and had I let Roscoe loose in the room there would most likely have been a small pile of feathers remaining when I returned! Shocked at the sight of one of the most prolific bird hunters I have ever seen, I screamed for Grace to help me. She came in and picked up Sparky as he was actually licking his lips at the sight of the small bird trapped within my fingers.

I double checked the room again before I allowed him to fly loose in the room.

A VERY close call!

Again he had several days to recuperate and he seemed quite happy to stay inside.He often would sit on my knee, shoulder or head whenever I would read or relax with him in the sunroom. If he was on some of his "perches" in the room and I stood up to leave he would fly and land on my shoulder or head in an obvious attempt to prevent me from leaving him, a technique that worked very well! He would nuzzle my ears and chew on my glasses or the chain I wear around my neck. It was getting much more difficult to contemplate releasing him again but I knew I had to try.

We also have a small flock of pet chickens. Chickens were never anything we planned to own but a strange set of events led us to them. We now have an automatic gate on our fence but when we had a manual one we simply left it open most of the time. Opening and closing it in the dark or rain was annoying and this was much easier. And so a strange tradition began.

For a number of years each Fourth of July, someone would abandon a ragged, toothless, decrepit old dog that would find its way through our gate to our front porch. It would live with us for a year and die the next Fourth of July and then another would find its way to us. One year it was a tiny tiny starving kitten. This poor miserable feline was so covered with fleas that it appeared to be mostly black but is actually a yellow tabby. When we rescued it, I rushed off to get a flea treatment while Grace fed the unfortunate creature a can of condensed milk. It was so hungry it cried the whole time it was eating what was probably its first meal in days. He survived and is still with us. He is practically brain dead but just the sweetest thing.

The following year we were joined by a one eyed rooster that we named Cogburn in honor of John Wayne's memorable character in the movie TRUE GRIT, the one eyed bounty hunter named ROOSTER COGBURN. For about a week I had heard him crowing and each day I knew he was getting closer and on the Fourth of July I saw him fly over the fence into our yard. He seemed to like it and settled in so I bought a few hens to keep him company. Thus our chicken days began. The lucky birds who live here can plan on dying of old age as they are beloved pets.

They free range all day and go into their coop at dusk to sleep, protected from raccoons and other predators. Their coop which I built, was once shown in CHICKENS magazine because of the unusual design. It's 4'x4'x8' and the bottom is wire. It's mounted on 4 large casters so I can easily move it around the yard after I thoroughly hose it out each morning. This keeps it clean and eliminates odors, flies and other issues and fertilizes the grass.

And so the next release involved me taking Roscoe, in the cat carrier, and placing the carrier on top of the coop in a strategic spot in the yard close to the blueberry thicket.

I opened the doors and expected him to immediately take wing.

But he didn't.

Instead he stayed in the carrier and showed no desire to leave it. So I went to the blueberry thicket and found a couple of early ripe berries and gave them to him and he ate them greedily. But he stayed in the carrier and showed no inclination to leave. Finally I reached into the carrier and gently cupped him in my hand and placed him at the doorway of the carrier.

He stood there and stared blankly into the sky with his beak open and a slight quivering to his body. I did not know at that time but this is an indicator of fear. I can still see him standing there and then his concentration was on me as he stared at my face with a blank expression and his beak half open. I still feel so guilty that I didn't take him back inside where I now believe he wanted to be.

Instead I nudged him off of the coop forcing him to fly away, into the trees. I went inside but made frequent trips outside to keep an eye on him. He stayed mainly in the blueberry thicket where I'm sure he gorged on ripe berries. Again we kept the cats prisoners in the house to ensure he faced no dangers from them.

BUT after a couple of hours, I again stepped out onto the porch and observed him high in one of the trees. He was just starting to really sing and he was in full voice and it was so sweet that I watched and listened to him for a minute and then I looked up into the sky.

 And my heart nearly stopped.

Circling above him was a red tailed hawk and I have no doubt it was observing Roscoe! My years of running are far past me but I relived the old days of my youth as I sprinted towards him shouting his name. I was also looking for something I might throw at the hawk to distract and hopefully frighten it away. Roscoe was far from the brilliant red color he would become but he was still very visible and his singing only added to the threat. Red tailed hawks are our primary aerial predator and are effective hunters. They dive on their prey of rodents, lizards, snakes and small birds with great efficiency and their razor sharp talons accurately pierce the bodies of their catches bringing almost immediate death and as quickly as they can they haul their meal to a nearby tree limb, the sharp beak neatly rips their victim's head off and they feast on it.

And I could see all of this happening in my head as I rushed towards him.

Happily the hawk decided I was not worth tangling with and veered away and Roscoe took to the air and flew directly to me. He then did something that he would repeat each time we released him after this . He flew right to me but instead of landing on my head or shoulder, he came so close to my head that I could feel the air turbulence from his wing tips on my cheek. He then headed to our customary pickup spot: the blueberry thicket.

Out of breath and my heart pounding, partially from the exertion of my out of shape old body, and partially from what I had barely prevented. I stumbled the rest of the way to my little buddy. Trying to catch my breath, I bent over at the waist wheezing noisily. When I was able to straighten up I saw he had already come into position for me to collect him and carry him inside to safety.

There were several other unsuccessful attempts to release him, each with their moments of concern. Once I saw a large rat snake working its way through the limbs of the thicket. It was on a collision course with Roscoe and it obviously was pursuing its next meal. It was concentrating on getting within range of the plump feathered snack and so it was unaware of me until I grabbed it behind its bullet shaped head and gently removed it from the limbs and as it wrapped itself around my arm, I carried it to our backyard and released it on the embankment leading to our creek. None the worse for wear, it quickly slithered into the underbrush where it would hunt frogs, squirrels, mice, birds...and other snakes.

I have always loved reptiles and especially snakes even though I once had a pet Water Moccasin, a very venomous snake, because I mistook it for an ordinary Water Snake. Although they can be very nasty, this one was easy to handle and I used to wear him around my neck, but once its identification was ensured I took it out into a swamp and released it.

Anyway, I saw Roscoe wanted to go inside after this near miss, and I took him to "his" room.

Roscoe began to venture away from the front yard. He began going into our neighbor's yard and sampling the delights found there. A holly tree was loaded with ripe red berries and he gorged on them. But mostly he stayed in our front yard.

Grace had not gotten too involved in Roscoe's care, leaving it to me. But on one of his forays outside she was standing on the front porch and two of our cats were with her. They were on the bannisters of the porch enjoying the vigorous petting she was administering to them. She looked up and saw Roscoe heading straight to her. Apparently he wanted to come inside and was going to her to be accomodated.

The cats also noticed he was coming in and prepared to snatch him as soon as he was in range. She started waving her arms to stop his progress. He veered off just in time and flew to a nearby tree. She grabbed two very disappointed felines and stuffed them inside the house and then walked over to him. He allowed her to hold him in her hands and carry him inside. I was so shocked when I saw her take him to the sunroom.

I was starting to think perhaps releasing him was not the right thing to do. It was obvious he was happy being with us and frankly I was really starting to worry about his safety. Everything wanted to eat him and it would only be a matter of time. I read that up to 80% of all fledglings do not survive the first year and the life expectancy of a Cardinal in the wild is about 2 years but in captivity, they can live up to 20 years.

What should I do?

The next time I released him I made a solemn vow to not go outside. That did not mean I couldn't stare out the windows to check on him and I did frequently but I never saw him. Perhaps his time had come.

But just before sunset I slipped out to close the chickens up in their coop and I kept looking into the trees and bushes but he was nowhere. I crisscrossed the yard looking and my heart steadily grew heavy. Finally I could not control myself and I called his name.

Nothing.

I called again and again, each time louder and louder. It started to grow dark and I slowly headed to the house. Then I called one last time.

Silence.

As I stepped onto our porch, from somewhere far away I heard it.

CHIRP!

I rushed back into the yard and called again. And I heard it!

CHIRP! CHIRP! CHIRP! CHIRP! CHIRP! **CHIRP!** **CHIRP! CHIRP!**

And then he burst out of the trees flying as fast as his wings would go and he saw me and dove down to my level and buzzed me but this time I actually felt the soft caress of his wingtips on my cheek as he headed into the blueberries and I rushed over and he quickly hopped down from branch to branch until he was at my level. He stood perfectly still, allowing me to capture him in my hands and I held him against my chest. I could feel the rapid beat of his heart and I'm sure he felt mine. And as I triumphantly carried him into the house, I made my decision.

He was going to live with us!

After all, shouldn't he have a voice in his life? He wanted to stay and I wanted him to stay.

Welcome to the Family!

If Roscoe was going to stay, a number of changes and adjustments needed to happen. The cat carrier would no longer suffice. He would need a cage. And a cage big enough to allow him to exercise and move about, although I had no intentions of him being a full time prisoner. Our sunroom is quite roomy and I wanted him to have the ability to spend most of his time free in it.

When I was about 10, I received a parakeet for my birthday and he was loose in my room most of the time. In the morning I would awaken to him gently pulling on my lower lip. He would land on my chest and hop up and wake me up. While I did homework or read a book he would sit on my head and chew on my hair or move to my shoulders and nibble my ear.

But a few years earlier I had received a male 'keet and then my brother received a female. Before long, Mike's bird laid an egg and our Dad became interested in the idea of breeding them. And so he built a big outdoor cage and included a few nesting boxes. It didn't take long before he had to build a much larger cage and put a large number of nesting boxes in and we learned that parakeets can breed like rats! We had so many birds that on a couple of occasions Dad would open the cage doors and shoo a dozen or two out. We had parakeets as part of our outdoor fauna for a number of years. And of course anybody who wanted one or two or a dozen were welcome to them. But finally the droppings and fallen seed attracted rats and Mom put her foot down. So one evening a truck and trailer pulled into our driveway and two men and my father struggled to load and tie down the cage on the trailer and we watched The Great Parakeet experiment disappear into the darkness.

Well I began looking for a cage for Roscoe. I visited pet stores and looked online for cages. I visited CraigsList, the Flea Markets and garage sales hoping to find a spacious cage and stand preferably at a reasonable price. But I was finding that I could get a good cage but at a higher than desired price or an affordable cage that would be damaged or rusty or missing parts. Like a door.

But none of them were at all spacious and that was the critical requirement. I was envisioning a parrot cage as the best I could hope for. But even that would not be what I really wanted for Roscoe.

And then we met Judy Carter.

Since Day One I had kept up a daily accounting of what we were going through on Facebook and a couple of other Cardinal related sites and forums. I was shocked at how many people love and adore Cardinals and Roscoe found a very interested audience. I shared the pain of trying to feed him and the joy of finally succeeding. His releases and returns were followed first by dozens and then hundreds and likely thousands. It seems that his audience included North America, South America, Australia and Europe. True proof of the power of social interactions.

And so I posted that I was looking for a cage and Judy came to our rescue. Judy, one of the many friends I had never met, sent me a message she had a cage I could have for free. Her son had kept a couple of ferrets in it and she said it was big. Since beggars can't be choosers, I gratefully accepted and Grace and I drove our Volvo XC90 to her house. The XC90 has a very large cargo area but we soon learned it wasn't big enough. When we pulled into her driveway we saw THE CAGE in the driveway. It was huge. Roscoe was being well set up.

We lowered the seats and Judy's husband managed to get it mostly into our vehicle.

Mostly.

The rear gate could not close and we were not prepared for this and all we could find to secure it was some thin string. Kite string and not much of it. Since we had an hour and a half highway trip ahead of us we realized this would never make it so we found a place to pull over and I managed to disassemble it and pack it into the car and we headed home.

Again, Judy, thank you so very much for your generosity. We are forever in your debt!

Once we got home, I dragged the pieces into the sunroom and began to assemble them. Immediately I saw a small issue in that there were no perches, only a couple of shelves that stretched the depth of the cage and were a foot wide. I played with various positions and usage and quickly realized I could use one to hold food and water cups but two would take up too much room. So I grabbed my keys and wallet and prepared to drive to the pet store to buy perches, although I thought finding the correct size might be difficult. As I marched to the car I saw a small branch lying on the ground. With so many trees we were always picking up deadfalls. I picked it up to toss into a compost pile when I saw this branch could make a decent perch. Inspiration hit me and I scoured the yard for more fallen limbs. I soon had a handful and I grabbed some pruning shears and twine from the garage and took them inside. Some quickly proved to be too short or too thin but there were several that could stretch across the cage or be fitted to connect two corners of the cage. I trimmed where necessary and fit them in place and took the twine and remembering my Boy Scout days, I lashed them in place after fitting each end between 2 separate bars of the cage. This would prevent them from slipping out of place as Roscoe perched on them.

I decided a few more would be good and so armed with lopping shears I went outside and cut branches from several trees and soon I had built a series of "stairways" that ran from a foot above the bottom of the cage on one side and three feet up from the other. There was adequate room for Roscoe to do short flights within the cage but basically he could hop up and down among the branches much like he would do inside a bush. I found a deep plastic bin which fit nicely under the end with the higher set of branches. This was stocked with live crickets and mealworms. Roscoe could drop in anytime he was hungry for a live treat. To give the crickets and mealworms a fighting chance I placed dried grasses, pine straw, twigs leaves and pine cones in the bin to give them hiding places and it would provide The Krimson Kid with some entertainment as he hunted for his meals.

And Roscoe had shown a real love for shiny things so I hung a number of costume jewelry, rings, chains, even an old watch and a collection of keys from the bars and limbs for him to enjoy. I even mounted a small bell on one thin limb that jingled whenever he jumped on it. He must have enjoyed it a lot as we heard the jingling frequently throughout the day.

Later I would add larger and taller limbs to the sides and top of the cage which curved up and over the top of the cage. This, The Penthouse, as we called it, expanded his kingdom even more.

While I was preparing the cage, Roscoe was confined to the cat carrier and I'm sure he somehow knew all of this was for him. He watched intently all phases of putting his new home together. He chirped and tweeted excitedly as if he was somehow encouraging my efforts and urging me to be finished.

I rolled the cage in front of the windows so he would be right next to the back door. One great advantage of this particular cage was that the pages of our local newspaper fit neatly on the floor of the cage and the single shelf that sat a foot below the ceiling of the cage on the right side. Also the shelves had holes at each corner and plastic pins that fit the holes. So I covered the shelf with newspaper and then secured it by pushing the pins through the holes. The last thing I did was to fill a shallow bowl with water and another with a mixture of seeds and put them on the shelf.

The cage had 3 sets of double doors that were stacked on top of each other vertically in the center of the cage. I closed the bottom one and then with small bungee cords I secured the top two sets in the open positions.

And then I opened the door of the cat carrier….

Roscoe stepped to the entrance of the carrier and threw himself at the cage!

He flew directly into it and landed on a limb. He hopped back and forth excitedly and paused long enough to chew on a shiny bracelet before continuing his explorations. He went from the center of the cage, up to the shelf where he examined the bowl of seeds and then started visiting each and every limb and branch inside the cage. Then he flew up to the cage doorway where he perched for a few seconds looking at his new world and then flew out, circled the room a couple of times before landing on the top bars of the cage and hopping back and forth across its expanse.

It was exactly like watching a young child experiencing their first Christmas morning, complete with lights, gifts and a tree. Joy and wonderment. Grace and I laughed, pointed and commented throughout the entire event. We were almost as excited as he was.

Almost…

A Comfortable Routine

Roscoe soon saw the cage as his personal space. Each morning at sunrise, as soon as I heard him stirring, I arose and went into the kitchen and fixed myself a cup of hot tea. As it brewed I gathered a cup of fresh water, his wax worms (from the refrigerator) and a couple of blueberries, blackberries, watermelon, or apple, whatever we had available. Then I would balance everything and enter the sunroom and place it all on the coffee table. I regularly purchased a live flowering plant that sat in a small bucket and I poured the contents of his water bowl into the plant and wiped the bowl clean with a paper towel and then refilled it from the cup I had brought in. I likewise dumped his seed bowl into a trash can and refilled the bowl from one of the several different collections of seed I had stored in airtight plastic containers. I'd take a sip of hot tea and put the cup on the armrest of the recliner in the corner and also take the top from the container of wax worms and select one before putting the container on the armrest next to my tea.

While I was doing this Roscoe would be eagerly hopping from perch to perch, waiting for me to open the doors to the cage. I would open the top two sets of double doors to the cage and secured both to the sides of the cage with small bungee cords. Once I was finished he would then hop onto the entrance of one of the sets of doors, usually the second one. He would then quiver like a puppy dog while I sang his good morning song which went like this (to the tune of Happy Birthday),

Good morning to you!

Good morning to you!

Good morning little twerp bird (or some other variation),

GOOD MORNING TO YOUUUUUUUUU!

Some of the variations to "his" song included "turd bucket", "pain in the butt", ``seed sucker", "cricket breath" and "birdy buddy".

Luckily nobody could hear me. I have no musical or singing abilities and at my best I sound like a bullfrog with a nasal issue. Luckily he didn't care and seemed to appreciate the effort and attention.

And then I gave him his first waxworm of the morning. Mostly he either stood there or retreated into the cage to eat his morsel but occasionally he would hop onto my shoulder or head to gulp his snack down. Then he would launch himself into the air and would do several laps of the room while I settled myself in the recliner, balancing my tea and the container of wax worms as I reclined back to a comfortable position.

Then he would land on the armrest and wait for me to fish out another worm and then he would hop over to take it. He would generally eat two to three more and then he would stop.. Then he would again circle the room zooming first high and then low. He would fly to the top of his cage and play among the perches I added there and then over to the live plants I put in the room and then to the coffee table for a sip of water or a couple of seeds or to chew on fresh flowers or a bit of fruit. Once he burned off that initial burst of energy he most often re-entered the cage.

The cage was his special sanctuary and hiding place. Kind of an avian Panic Room. If there was a loud unexpected noise or if he heard a hawk scream from outside, he would scoot into the cage and would "hide" in the corner on a perch. But soon he would again sit in the doorway and peer outside of the cage to make sure all was well. He would look right, then left, up and down. Then he would look at me apparently for confirmation that it was safe to leave his cage. I liked the fact that he was so cautious. The idea of another attempt at releasing him or an accidental release was always in my mind and I wanted him as ready to survive as possible.

Inside Flight

Flying is a bird's primary source of exercise and I was briefly worried by how much Roscoe was getting. Our sunroom is very roomy but when the house next door came on the market, we seriously considered buying it for two reasons. First it has a 5 car garage compared to our 3 car garage. As tempting as that was, I realized having more space to store junk was no reason to go into debt.

But it had a massive sunroom that ran the width of the house and like our sunroom, has a breathtaking view of the river and marshes behind us. I often fantasized about what we could do with that room. Especially what it could do for Roscoe as it would easily quadruple his flying space. But again, going into debt is something we both abhor and so we decided to stay in our house that we love so much.

And it's a good thing too! A couple from North Carolina bought it and they moved in three weeks before Hurricane Michael developed. At 5:00am, a tornado hit their house after knocking down 9 big oak trees. It ripped that sunroom completely off of the house, carried it over their roof (while causing extensive roof damage) and then dumped it in OUR front yard while knocking down 4 of our trees. We were trapped for 2 days.

So we got that sunroom for FREE, but not at all the way we wanted it. In fact we had to pay to have the trees and the flattened sunroom removed. Rats.

But I soon learned I need not worry about Roscoe's ability to get his exercise. He had his own methods.

He often flew in circular paths within the confines of the room but then he started flying into the walls and windows with a loud BANG! I was very concerned that he would injure himself but this was my first hint of how very intelligent he was.

When he would do this I would cringe and worry that he would fall after such an impact and crash onto the floor or furniture but he never did. Nor did he stop flying. It took a lot of careful observation to realize what he was doing. He had learned exactly how much room he had within the 4 walls and he was banking off of the walls exactly as a competitive swimmer banks off the walls of a pool so he can swiftly reverse course and swim towards the opposite wall. He would fly straight at the wall at full speed but just before crashing, he reversed course and pushed away from the wall with his feet and legs! It was hard to see because it happened so fast and you had to be standing in just the right spot to see what he was doing. I only caught it a couple of times. Once I did, I relaxed while he did it. But it was impressive! VERY impressive!

Another trick he taught himself was to fly nonstop BEHIND the recliner and the lamp beside it and then behind the cage. The recliner, about halfway down the back, above the seat, has a bow to it that leaves a gap of less than a foot from the wall behind it. But Grace insists that I pull it away from the wall another 6 or so inches so it doesn't hit the wall when I lean back.

There is a pole lamp beside it and the pole bends towards the wall. The cage also sat a foot away from the windows next to it.

So this Evel Knevel of birds would zip towards the recliner and lamp and without losing a wing stroke would fly AT FULL SPEED behind the furniture and emerge from the other side. Because it was placed diagonally at a corner of the room there was more space behind it that may have helped him perform this breakneck trick. He would fly alongside the wall and bank and go behind the cage.

If you watched the Star Wars series of movies you saw young Anakin Skywalker run his pod racer in **Episode 1**, **THE PHANTOM MENACE**. This was eerily similar.

Cleanliness is Next to Godliness

A bird in the house is, well, messy. Initially so was Roscoe.

I've referred to his love of baths and maybe this came from his early times with us. I described my difficulties in feeding him because of my vision issues and a fear of causing severe bodily harm to him by shoving a food covered finger deep into his craw and maybe harming his delicate internal organs or causing his tiny beak to fall apart from the brute force of a finger causing them to pop right off. However none of that happened and soon I was driving his nutrients fast, hard and accurately into his throat. He seemed to appreciate the effort and would swiftly swallow and then open his beak for more,

But still bits and pieces would fly off or dribble down his chest and invariably turn his feathers into a crusty nasty coating. I'd wipe his feathers with a damp paper towel to clean him up a bit but I never got the impression he truly enjoyed the experience.

And so I placed a small shallow bowl of water on the coffee table for him and the first time he hopped into it, I knew he was intrigued by the feeling and possibilities. He hopped back and forth like a small child in a wading pool, then he bent forward slightly putting his beak into the water but instead of taking a drink, he made the water fly. It splashed over his head and his back and his wings beat the surface of the water furiously which threw up more water. Some of it landed on the bathing birdy but more flew onto the tabletop and all of its contents as well as on the floor.I sat down and enjoyed the show but mostly I enjoyed his reaction to his first bath. It was pure and simple joy!

I remembered our son Chad and his early experiences in water. As a newborn, Grace would put him in the kitchen sink with warm water and he loved it. She fed him there, then bathed him so it was easier to clean him up and he cooed and giggled throughout it.

But soon he outgrew the sink and bath time duties were passed on to me. We had a massive old tub and I would fill it with warm water and then slip in and Grace would pass him to me and soon he'd be clean, pink and as slick as a baby seal. Then it was Daddy and Son playtime and would end up with my son resting on my chest as I held him. It was one of my very best experiences and memories. One time he was so delirious with pleasure he began to spin in the water laughing and cooing. Grace commented it looked as if he was performing in a water ballet! I enjoyed the experience as much as he did. Bath time was a wonderful daily ritual.

Except for one time!

I was leaning back in the tub as he lay on my chest and I was enjoying the sensation of his body on mine. And then I noticed we were NOT alone.

Grace was at the far end of the house when she heard my blood curdling scream. "**GRACEEEEEEEE!**"

She came running to whatever catastrophe had beset us. The tub was draining and I had sat up and was holding our only offspring high in the air away from danger. I practically threw him to her as I sprang up and jumped out of the tub. She screamed in panic, "What happened? What's wrong?"

I pointed down at the tub.

One of the best parts of the movie CADDYSHACK, was when a kid throws a chocolate candy bar into a pool full of people. It creates a panic as people try to escape what appears to be a floating ....turd. This was exactly like that except it wasn't a candy bar I saw drifting in the tub with us. As described in the movie, Chad had released a doody.

Like in the movie, the tub required a serious cleaning.

And so little birds are a lot like little human children. They eat a lot, spill a lot, leave things behind for others to clean up. They are noisy, nosy, shy when you wish they would be friendly and gregarious when it's best that they be silent.

Come to think about it, little birds are a lot like teenaged humans and a number of mature and elderly adults. Challenging.

Well Roscoe started out like this. He would wolf down morsels of food and whatever did not easily go down his piehole he would simply break off the portions that did and let the rest fall. And the worst was if his beak got dirty the solution was to simply wipe it off. On whatever was convenient, such as the tabletop, the floor or carpet, the bars of his cage or....ME!

He had no issues wiping his dirty, greasy, worm juice covered beak on my clothing, skin or hair. Being with him demanded good grooming habits. On the plus side, it seems worm juice makes an excellent hair conditioner. You may quote me, Martha Stewart!

Also the seed hulls, chewed up blades of grass or masticulated cricket legs and grape stems seemed to offend his senses of priority when they cluttered up the coffee table top and he would pick them up and toss them over the side to the floor below. Likewise any "toy" he tired of playing with such as bells or straws must also be eliminated from His Highness' sight. Pick them up and place them back on the table and he would practically break his neck to swoop on them and gleefully kick them over the side. Cats do the same. Both are irritating.

Well Grace and I divide up the household chores. I vacuum and mop, take care of the windows and occasionally cook plus I do ALL of the outdoor jobs which include mowing, edging, leaf cleanup (a full time job by itself), pressure washing and more. Grace handles the bills, laundry and most kitchen duties. However no discussion was necessary about what needed to be done inside the sunroom. It was ALL my responsibility. I brought him home and no matter how much Grace loved him, EVERYTHING related to him was my job.

And I didn't mind.

The time I had with him was magical and even scrubbing the floors was fun. For one reason I NEVER did anything alone. He was always in the middle of what I was doing. It was like having a mmsmall feathered 4 year old human child with me. He didn't ask the incessant questions of a small child but he insisted on "helping" with everything I did. Often he would undo what I had just cleaned. He would sit on the rim of the garbage can I brought in and he would pull the newspapers I had just dumped back out, spilling all of the contents I had carefully collected and wrapped up all over the floor. He might spy some little forgotten treasure sitting at the bottom of the can and he would drop in to save it and stuff would stick to his feathers and he would fluff his feathers from a high perch and the dust and chaff would float through the air until it landed on the floor I had just mopped. And I always emptied and refilled his seed bowl and he seemed to relish throwing the new seeds all over the table top and then onto the just cleaned floor below.

My favorite event would be when I'd be on my hands and knees, crawling across the floor scrubbing his fecal materials away. He would either hop along with me between my hands, chirping merrily as he pointed out the spots I had missed or he would ride on my back or head singing merrily and bragging about his human slave whom he could ride whenever he wanted. I would swat him away and he would fly off and circle the room once or twice before returning to the same spot.

I doubt I enjoyed it as much as he did.

But it was close.

Now we must discuss the biggest issue of allowing a bird to be loose within a house. The dreaded BIRDIE BOMBS. SPARROW SPLATTER. PIGEON STATUE PLOPPERS. ROBIN ROUNDS. CROW CLUSTER BOMBS. MOCKINGBIRD MUCK. HUMMINGBIRD HILLS. CARDINAL CA-CA. Those black and white mini mounds that dotted the interior landscape.

Now I had always understood that birds do not have a muscled sphincter as we do which means they have no bowel control. And so wherever they go, they go! But it seems they do have muscles around their cloaca, which is their "everything exits" portal which is where they release feces and eggs. But they do have a rectocoprodeal sphincter which allows a small amount of control, but very little. And the frequency of how often birds evacuate their bowels is a matter of the size of the bird. Small birds empty themselves about every 10 minutes because the lighter the body the faster they can fly. So remember this the next time your car's windshield requires cleaning. (Bet this was NOT a subject you expected to read about when you started reading this, did you?)

Luckily their fecal material is pretty easy to clean up. I'd wipe down any decorated areas with a damp cloth which effectively removed the droppings. Then I would spray a mixture of Simple Green (I love the smell of it) and water over the area and wipe it down again. I would do this every other day and watch where I sat on the secondary days.

BUT I began to notice that I was cleaning up less and less and I was initially concerned that perhaps he wasn't eating as much and perhaps was getting ill. However it certainly appeared that he was eating as much, his energy level remained high, his eyes were still clear and bright and he was continuing to grow and fill out.

But I was definitely cleaning up fewer droppings and the number continued to dwindle. Grace also noticed and commented on this. Something was happening but what?

Not long after we noticed the decrease in his fecal gifts, he was perched on my chest happily pecking at my beard when suddenly he stopped. A strange look seemed to appear on his face and then he flew from me and made a straight line dash to the inside of his cage. He landed on a perch and hopped to another and then stood still. Then I saw him shiver slightly and lift his tail feathers and then a REDBIRD ROUNDER dropped from his backside and onto the newspaper at the bottom of the cage. He then flew back to me and continued searching for treasure within my facial hair.

I was stunned! Did I really see him avoiding voiding his bowels on me? In truth he rarely soiled me but this appeared to be a deliberate move to not desecrate me. Had he actually housebroken himself? Was he anticipating his need to relieve himself and placing it where it was no longer a problem? Had he observed my efforts to clean up behind him and was consciously assisting me? Was everything I thought I knew about birds' digestive tracts and elimination process wrong?

I can't say but from that point forward I saw him do this numerous times and I rarely had much to clean up after him. I wish I knew the answer.

There was a pole lamp that stood next to the recliner and he loved to stand on the top of it, usually when I sat in the recliner below him. Apparently this spot was NOT included in the "housebroken zone" and its black surface was usually polka dotted with white/ black clumps. It was a small surface so a wet sponge and a few swipes and it was clean again.

Note: Some readers may have some serious doubts about my statements concerning Roscoe's toilet training. I DO NOT BLAME YOU! I always believed a bird physically could not restrict or control its elimination process. I did share with a few people, some of whom had birds as pets or a food supply (chickens and ducks) and those with birds in their lives either gave me questioning looks or openly scoffed at me.

I debated including that part in the book, fearing people would not believe it and then doubt other parts of this book. But I went ahead and put it in.

But as I am writing this, there is a chicken in a cat carrier in a chair beside me. Her name is Tilly, she's our "senior" chicken. She is a Jersey Giant, a breed that has black feathers, black skin and is larger than most breeds, often resembling a short black turkey. Tilley is our third Jersey Giant. Originally we had Large Marge and Big Ass Bertha. Bertha died so we got Two Ton Tilley to keep Marge company. We've found that chickens will often form friendships with members of their own breed and like to pair them when possible. Sadly when Marge died we haven't been able to find her a companion.

Well Tilley is ill. She has an eye infection which has shut her right eye completely and because of this the other members of the flock pick on her and chase her away from the food and the coop. By the time I realized what was happening she weighed hardly anything. So we began bringing her in at night.

Secured in the carrier we stuff her full of food and she sleeps in the kitchen until morning when we again feed her and we leave her in the box until after the other chickens are released and fed and then begin their daily tours of the property where they search for tasty bugs, worms and seed.

When the coast is clear, Tilley is taken outside and released.

But on several occasions the normally taciturn Jersey Giant will start "talking". First it will be an almost inaudible string of low clucks. If we don't react then the volume and cadence will increase and continue until she is practically screaming at us. If for any reason we do not take her carrier outside, she will foul the box with a watery blast of chicken excrement. But if we act before she starts trying to talk to us or shortly after, she will exit the box and waddle a short distance before emptying her bowels.

Tilley is basically doing the same thing Roscoe did so many times! She is controlling her bowels until she is in a "safe" spot before letting Nature take its course. I'm sure she doesn't want to be "cooped up" in the tight confines of the carrier with her own filth.

Gender Wars

I posted nearly daily pictures and videos of my boy. Facebook, Nextdoor, a local forum and Cardinal Cottage were my usual spots to share Roscoe with the world. Soon he had friends and fans on four continents and many people told me their daily "dose" of Roscoe was a blessing for them. They enjoyed my trials and tribulations with The Krimson Kid and apparently shared them with others and his popularity grew. Cardinals are a favorite bird of many people and the stories, photos and videos were a big hit.

But there was one issue that people debated, disagreed and argued over: his gender.

People would tell me I needed to give him a new name, one more appropriate for a female Cardinal. Roscoe was still primarily brown but the red coloring was rapidly developing. I advised people that It might take as long as a year for the males' red coloring to develop and I explained that the photos and videos were done on my iPad and in the natural sunlight or whatever light bulbs we had available and it was possible his coloring was not coming through. I promised everyone that My Boy was actually a male. And even if he was a she, I named him Roscoe and I liked it and he would stay Roscoe.

He may have lost a few friends because of my attitude, but I seriously doubt it. He was just too cute.

And, of course, I was right!

I Don't Like You Anymore!

We have some friends who live in Macon, Georgia, Lyle and Linda Brooks. Lyle and I worked together for a number of years. Right after Lyle started with the work group I was in, we had a conference / Christmas party in Atlanta and we stayed at Callaway Gardens. The wives were invited as well and after the Christmas party, we joined a group that headed out into the Gardens. They had a train ride on an open air steam train to see "a major display of lights and decorations" and everybody wanted to ride on it. There were two remaining trips for the night but too many people jumped in for the first trip and the four of us didn't make it on. So we waited an hour and a half in the bitter cold for the train to return and we talked and shivered and a friendship formed between the four of us. The train returned and we joined the small crowd that also waited. On the hard wooden seats we quickly realized it was colder in the train than outside! And as we rode the route, the open windows funneled in even more frigid air, making it a far from magical Christmas experience. Add to that the "major display of lights and decorations" was a very cruel exaggeration. There would be a small display of lights and then nothing for several minutes. Then maybe a lighted inflatable snowman all by himself and then again an extended time and distance with nothing to see.

Luckily they decided to not charge us for the ride, because I would have demanded a refund.

But it is shared experiences, good and bad, that forges real friendships and so the experience was actually valuable because our friendships have lasted many years.

Lyle and Linda own a couple of vacation time shares, and they often invited us to join them. One of our favorites is at Ormond Beach, Florida, less than 100 miles away from our home. And we were scheduled to go down and spend a week with them.

I was really looking forward to the trip. During the day, Lyle and I would metal detect the beach, searching for buried treasures and Grace and Linda played Bingo, swam in the pool and yakked between themselves. At night we cooked fabulous meals then played Dominoes. It always was a glorious week. But there was only one issue: Roscoe.

I was worried about leaving him alone for a week. He was not used to solitude, plus he would need fresh water and food. I considered asking a neighbor to look in on him and take care of him but the one I could ask has several small grandchildren and they love to come to our place and help care for our chickens. And I know they would want to come in and see Roscoe. Under normal circumstances they were always welcome, but I would not be there to supervise and make sure that none of the cats slipped into Roscoe's room or that he didn't slip out into their space. And they are great kids and very gentle and loving but accidents happen and I could easily imagine their enthusiasm and a small delicate bird resulting in a real tragedy.

Another alternative was my son, Chad. Chad loves all animals and especially our cats. You see OUR cats were once HIS cats. But when he went to Australia for three years to study music ministry at Hillsong College, they stayed with us. The once "inside cats" became "outside cats" and we decided it was best if they continued to live with us. So I knew he would make all efforts to make the long drive to our house to care for his former pets.

BUT Roscoe was another matter.

Chad loves all animals but he had a very busy work schedule, often putting in 80 to 100 hours a week. I asked him to give Roscoe some attention as I knew he would be lonely and Chad promised he would. Mid week he posted a picture of his head with Roscoe perched in his hair and the caption "STUPID BIRD!". But he was only able to get up there a few times and mostly after dark and Roscoe would be asleep in his cage. Chad would quickly freshen his water and seed and then scoot out of the room to play with "his" cats before making the long drive back to his house.

And so Roscoe spent what was basically a lonesome week by himself and he started to revert towards being wild. And when we came home the first thing I did was to eagerly take some waxworms to his room and offer them to him. I expected him to fly straight to me if only to enjoy his snack but it didn't happen. In fact he acted like he did not know me and did not trust me at all. He flew to the opposite part of the room to a high perch and stayed there. If I approached him, he immediately relocated as far away from me as possible. I was getting the cold shoulder.

Then I sat in the recliner with my container of wax worms and one or two in my extended open palm and waited for him to warm up to me or at least get hungry enough to come and get a quick and tasty meal.

But he didn't.

After a couple of hours, I placed a few wax worms in a bowl on the coffee table and left the room. A few hours later I reentered the room and he again fled away from me. I did notice the wax worms were gone so he wasn't sick, which was a relief.

I quietly sat in the recliner and read a book while keeping an eye on him. After a while I again left the room and did not return until he had gone into the cage for the night. I closed the cage doors and left him alone.

Two can play this game.

But the next morning I went in and opened the cage doors and waited for him to fly to the entrance of the cage as he had done every morning since moving into it. Then I would sing to him and slip him a fat waxworm. Just like before we went on vacation. And all would be forgiven and forgotten.

But he didn't. He stayed in the cage, still as far away from me as possible. Once I moved back he quickly went to the cage entrance and then flew out and again was as far from my presence as possible. I sat in the recliner hoping for him to come to me. After an hour I left.

This became the routine for about 3 weeks. I was initially puzzled by his behavior but eventually I became angry over it. Many times I was tempted to open the exterior door of the sunroom and drive him out and away. Many, many times. But the weather was starting to change and I could not justify that action. I would have to wait until spring before sending the ungrateful little bastard on his way.

They say "Hell hath no fury, like a woman scorned!" but I can vouch that a pissed off Cardinal runs a close second place!

Other times I sat and stared at him in dismay. I tried bribery of every kind to draw him down but whatever prize I offered was refused. I even thought of catching him with a net and forcibly holding him in my hands in the hopes it might revive our lost friendship, but I was afraid of making the situation even worse, so I did not.

Finally I came to the conclusion I had blown it. I should have driven back every other day to care for him and spend time with him or possibly not gone on our vacation. I would have had an angry wife and two upset friends, but at least I would still be in Roscoe's good graces.

I continued to sit with him and read or simply stare out of the windows. Often I would watch him as he watched me but always from a distance.

Stalemate.

After nearly a month passed with no sign of rekindling my relationship with my former birdie buddy, the occasion of cleaning his room came around again. As I described earlier, he would be an enjoyable pest, distracting me with his antics by getting in the way and undoing my efforts. But since our ill fated vacation, he had snubbed me while I performed my household duties as house slave. He stayed as far away as space allowed. He continued the recent trend of sullenly staring down on me from his highest perches.

Well one morning I completed the room cleaning then I scrubbed and refilled his water and seed bowls. I hung a new millet stalk inside the cage and restocked his worm and cricket pan. I went outside and picked fresh grass and flowers for him and thinly sliced up a grape for him.

When I was done I went to sit on the loveseat and read but I became very tired and I stretched out as best as I could and closed my eyes and drifted away.

I have no idea how long I slept but I awoke to the familiar sensation of little bird feet hopping on my legs.

HOP!

HOPHOPHOP!

HOP!

HOPHOPHOPHOP!

I kept my eyes closed as I felt him working his way up my legs and onto my chest. I also tried to control my breathing as he slowly worked his way to my face.

HOP! HOPHOP! HOP!

Then I felt him gently picking at the facial hairs of my beard. I have never known if this was just a game he played with me, a gesture of affection or if he was seeking tiny morsels of food.

Then I felt him gently pecking at my lips. Bird kisses.

I ever so slightly peeked as he hopped onto my chin and began picking at my mustache hairs. A tear formed at the corners of my eyes as this was the welcome home I had yearned for and missed so much.

And then he did something unexpected, something he had never done before nor after. He shoved his beak deep inside my right nostril and grabbed a nasal hair and yanked. **HARD!**

I yelped in pain and half sat up swatting him away. He flew around the room twice but came back and landed on my shoulder and started gently nibbling on my ear, just like he used to do. I sat up completely and he flew up to my head and landed there and began playing with my hair. .

My eyes were watering from the pain of his "Booger Mining" but there were tears of joy mixed in. I slowly reached over to the container of wax worms on the coffee table. Moving slowly and deliberately so as to not spook him into flying away, I pulled out a particularly fat one and held it in my open palm resting on my leg. He quickly spied it and dropped onto my arm and hopped over and claimed his reward. Two more were happily accepted before he flew into his cage and began his morning bath. He was particularly energetic and threw water all over the windows and floor I had just cleaned.

The inside of my right nostril was quite tender for much of that day and I constantly heard him do what could only be bird giggles.

But I didn't mind.

My little crimson buddy was back.

I was forgiven.

But I've always wondered if that nasal attack was an innocent act or a form of punishment for leaving him alone for that week.

Tricks and Toys

Crows have long been recognized for their intelligence and problem solving skills. Well after seeing what Roscoe was able to do I must consider the Cardinals as major competition for any intelligence titles. Roscoe would see something he wanted or wanted to do and would study and experiment until he accomplished his task. His ability to concentrate on analyzing a situation or solving a puzzle was awesome.

Consider the bracelet and the necklace:

Shiny Things

Roscoe loved anything shiny and he had so many things to play with in his cage it looked like a small jewelry store. My mother had a bunch of beautiful pieces of costume jewelry so I had a steady supply of things for him to chew on and play with. But I hit upon a combination that amused him and anybody watching. And it proved how very intelligent he was.

I found a medium thickness silver necklace and a solid silver bracelet in Mom's stuff. I had placed a small bird swing hanging from the top of the cage for him to enjoy but he refused to have anything to do with it. As a child I had a pet parakeet who loved to swing on a similar one so when I saw it at the pet store I bought it immediately. I felt that if Roscoe would only perch on it for a few seconds he would enjoy the sensation of swinging back and forth. I tried everything possible to trick him to get on it. I hung his beloved millet stalks from the top bars of the cage so he could only reach them by balancing on the swing. He refused to even try and forgo his favorite treat. And so I thought he would certainly want to play with these new shiny toys so I hung them right beside the swing. I ran the necklace through the bracelet and then through the bars at the top of his cage where the bracelet hung down next to the swing. The only way he would be able to play with the bracelet was to either hang upside down from the inside of the cage or to perch on the swing. The clasp was a simple male/female connector but strong enough to hold the pieces together. I left the room shortly after connecting them and when I returned both were at the bottom of the cage.

I put them back in place and again left.

When I came back they were again at the bottom of the cage. I put them back.

After several more episodes like this I suspected something might be amiss. The clasp was surely strong enough that it should not easily part. So I put them up once more and sat in the chair. Moments later Roscoe flew to the top of the cage and easily popped the clasp open. Round one went to the bird.

"Okay!" I thought, "I'll show you." I then put them back in place but then pulled the necklace until the clasp was at the bottom of the loop. Then I sat on the couch and waited for the show. I fully expected him to look for the clasp and be unable to reach it and then maybe enter the cage and finally sit on the swing in order to reach the clasp.

I was disappointed. And thrilled.

The little turd landed and as expected, looked for the clasp. He hopped back and forth looking for it and then saw it dangling about 6 inches below the top of the cage. Quickly he realized he could not get to it. At least not as he had before.

So he set to work.

There is an expression: "If the mountain will not come to Muhammad, then Muhammad must go to the mountain". He proved that point.

He stood over the point where the necklace ran through the top bars of the cage, reached down and grabbed the chain in his beak and heaved up and over. When he did that the clasp began to move up towards him. He then grabbed the chain again and heaved it up and over once more. He continued to do this until the clasp traveled up to the top bars and then over and then he grabbed it and popped it free. He gave me a look that could only express victory and disdain for my puny human efforts to outsmart him! Round two and a knockout for The Feathered One!

I was mesmerized. And so proud.

I jumped up and reset it and he promptly did it again. If the clasp began to slide back down he would put one foot on the chain to stop its descent. Then it would soon be going upward again. Then it would crash onto the bottom of the cage.

Truly amazing.

I took many photos and videos of him but whenever I wanted to video him doing this he for some reason became camera shy and wouldn't "perform". I have only one video of this and it's not great but you can clearly see what he was doing. Because I was recording him he would stop and start and it took several minutes for him to complete it. However, one time when I was not videoing it he completed the whole thing in about 15 seconds.

Genius.

Roscoe loved any shiny objects and would do whatever was necessary to obtain them. I had a nurse, Tonya, who came monthly to the house to administer an infusion of antibodies that helped me control an autoimmune disease called Myasthenia gravis. After the treatment was completed she would always want to go visit Roscoe in the sunroom. Roscoe loved visitors but he seemed to particularly enjoy Tonya's visits.

Because she had pens!

She always had a ballpoint pen or two in her breast pocket and Roscoe loved to slip them free and try to fly away with them. But Tonya soon learned how to defend her property so whenever she entered the room, Roscoe would not wait for her to sit down before launching his attack. Instead he would immediately fly to her and snatch the pen while in mid flight. He became quite adroit at pulling them from her pocket but always ran into a snag in that he never could remove them where they were balanced in his beak and the uneven weight would cause them to slip from his grasp and fall to the floor where they were easily recovered by the rightful owner. Nonplussed, he would then wait until she sat down and then he would land on her arm and then again try to steal it. But Tonya would block his efforts of thievery and hold on to her writing tools. He would often then settle for landing on her head and mussing up her hair.

She didn't mind a bit. She, like everybody else, enjoyed his attention.

Straws

Another "trick" of his was an attraction to drinking straws, especially mine. Many times I would enter into the sunroom and settle down in the recliner with a fountain drink from a restaurant and usually there would be a lid with a straw poking out of the lid. I would place the cup on the floor beside the recliner and start to read a book or magazine. Without looking I would reach down to retrieve the cup and instead grasp a warm feathered body that would let out a surprised squawk and maybe give my hand a peck. While I wasn't looking, Roscoe would fly down and land on the lid of the cup and then proceed to try and remove the straw which he would then fly away with. Now this sounds like it would be easy to accomplish but if you looked at his size and the angle he would have to accomplish to remove the straw you would realize this was actually a Herculean task. Often these were large or extra large cups with very long straws that went all the way to the bottom of the cup and with only an inch or two of straw coming out.

He would have to grasp the straw in his beak and then lift up as far as he could go. If the lid opening was fairly large sized then the straw would simply slide back into the cup when he let go but if the opening was just large enough for the straw to enter but small enough to be a tight fit, then he could often lift the straw a bit and then quickly grasp it as low as possible and by lifting again the straw would be an inch or two higher. Repeat. Repeat. Repeat. Eventually he would actually raise it enough to topple out of the cup and he would have his prize. He was often so dedicated that I would find my drink no longer had a straw for me to sip through.

Peekaboo! I Hate You!

Go to any pet store and look at the selection of bird toys and you are likely to find mirrors. Most are made to be hung from the bars of a cage so the bird can enjoy its reflection and think it's with another bird. My pet parakeet, when I was a boy, loved to look in the mirror we placed in his cage. He would gaze at it for hours while cooing gently at it and trying to give it "kisses" with its beak. Some of our pet chickens will stand in front of a glass door and admire their reflection and cuddle up against it.

And so I bought Roscoe a mirror.

I hung it inside his cage by a perch and he went to investigate it. But when he saw his own reflection he let out a birdy scream! I believe it was a combination of fear and horror with a healthy dose of anger and rage. He then attacked his reflection, obviously trying to peck it and drive the strange flat bird away! I watched in fascination for a few moments before taking it away.

I put it on the coffee table so I could toss it away but forgot about it and on occasions he must have been snacking on the seed, fruit or flowers I put there for him and then hopped to where it lay. I would then hear that strange scream and upon entering the sunroom he would be as far away from the mirror as he could be, usually in the cage or on top of it and he would be staring at the spot where the mirror lay. I left it to see if he would accept the mirror but he never did and finally I threw it into the trash.

Then one morning I was sitting in the recliner, gazing out of the windows enjoying the view. In a nearby shrub a male and female Cardinal were snacking on some berries from the plant. Roscoe either did not see them or was ignoring their presence. He flew down to the floor and was playing with a twig when the female flew to the railing of our small deck, just outside of the sunroom. She hopped back and forth on it before approaching the glass windows and peering inside. It was at that precise moment that Roscoe flew up from the floor to the window sill and was face to face with her. Only the thickness of the glass separated them.

He then let out a mighty scream at this stranger. I'm not sure if her unexpected appearance frightened him or he was enraged and trying to frighten her away or both. However it did not faze her at all and she made no move to leave. He then screamed a second time before flying to me and landing on my shoulder and then looking balefully at his unwanted visitor.

I was reminded of his second release when he flew straight up into a tall tree and landed on a large branch. Immediately a pair of Mockingbirds knocked him off of the limb and as soon as he returned to his perch a male and female Cardinal also attacked him. He immediately fled, flying straight back to me for safety and protection.

Maybe he was destined to be a feathered hermit in the outside world.

The Ultimate Trick!

One time I went inside "his" room and saw he was playing with something. Curious, I grabbed him and pulled a thumbtack from his beak. I was shocked that he had it and wondered where he found it. Then I saw the source.

On one of the walls, I have a topographical map of the area which clearly identifies our location on Lofton Creek. It's held in place with a series of thumbtacks. Clearly this came from there as I could see the spot where it had been removed. What I couldn't see was HOW he managed to do so as there was no place for him to access it. Literally there was no place for him to land near it nor a place to reach it. The tacks were all securely pushed into place in the cedar paneling and he would no doubt struggle to free it.

A true mystery.

Now let me explain the area where this map is placed. I have a red leather recliner that sits in front of a corner in the room. The map is on one of the walls forming the corner. The room is decorated in a fisherman's motiff. An antique six horsepower outboard motor hangs on one wall (my father bought it when I was six months old) and numerous pictures, carvings, signs and fishing rods adorn the walls. Hanging vertically about six inches away from the map is my very first fishing rod and reel, an old Zebco reel and rod.

I returned Roscoe's thumbtack to the spot where it had been and sat in the recliner.

Soon he landed on the arm of the recliner and gave me a very dirty look for taking his toy away. He then hopped onto the reel and started to climb up the rod but he was perpendicular to it. Truly I have never seen nor heard of a bird doing this but he literally scooted upward in this style so it seems he had practiced the move! A woodpecker can move up and down a tree by grasping the bark, but Roscoe was traveling vertically, while his body was practically horizontal, on a smooth surfaced fishing rod and only the strength of his feet and legs supported him. He continued up the rod until he got to the appropriate spot and then BEGAN TO FLAP HIS WINGS FURIOUSLY! He and the fishing rod began to move towards the map and the thumbtack he had just lost! He basically flew with the rod over to the map and still holding on with his feet, grabbed the thumbtack in his beak! He now could stop flapping his wings as he was securely anchored in place and then he began to twist and tug the tack with his beak until it popped free from the wall and as it came free he released his hold on the fishing rod. He then flew himself with his prize into his cage and resumed playing with it.

I was frozen in place, unable to move or speak, as I tried to fully comprehend what I had just witnessed. The brilliance! The intelligence! I only wished I had somebody there to collaborate on what he did or to have videotaped it. Also the fact that he knew exactly where to stop climbing up the fishing rod told me he had likely experimented numerous times to learn how high he needed to travel to the exact spot that would allow him to reach his prize.

Also the determination and strength he exhibited because he was basically "flying" and dragging the weight of both the rod and the fishing reel in order to reach that thumbtack.

That was the only time I saw him do that as I again wrestled the tack from him but used a hammer to drive all of the tacks deeper into the wood. Now he was unable to remove it again.

It remains one of my favorite memories.

Roscoe's Christmas Tree

Christmas has always been our favorite time of year. And we especially loved Christmas trees!

Our first house was a tiny bungalow with a lot of charm. Two bedrooms, one bathroom, Great room and kitchen. But it had a wrap-around front porch with a swing, hardwood floors and a fireplace that smoked constantly, it was a favorite of everybody who entered. We would throw Christmas parties that had over 100 people shoulder to shoulder in it and people crammed onto the porch.

In fact we closed on the sale of it in July and immediately invited friends over. We rolled up the horribly ugly carpet that covered the floors, turned the air conditioning down low and built a fire in the fireplace and marvelled at it all. While hacking from the chimney smoke.

At Christmas, I decided to go into the woods, find the perfect tree, dig it up and plant it into a bucket. After Christmas I would plant it in the yard as a remembrance of our first Christmas as man and wife.

What a stupid idea!

First of all, you need to know we have Southern Pine trees that are not at all like a typical Christmas tree. The limbs grow haphazardly and there are usually great spaces between them. They also have a primary taproot that is as long as the tree is tall. So a four foot tree has a four foot root. Not an easy task to dig up!

After trekking around in the woods for several hours, I was tired and dirty and still looking for that "perfect tree" and decided to settle for something less than perfect. I made several attempts to dig trees but would give up after that long strong root seemed to just keep going, possibly all the way to China.

I kept going to smaller and smaller trees until finally I picked one and when I got down about three feet deep and the root was still descending I whacked the root repeatedly with the edge of my shovel until I got to the point where I simply wrestled with it until the root snapped. I dragged it to my car and then struggled to get it inside, smearing pine sap all over my seats, dashboard and head liner. Pine sap is extremely sticky and virtually impossible to remove. I would eventually sell this car for almost nothing in order to escape the sap.

When I got home I took a five gallon bucket and crammed the root (what was left of it) in and then dug a hole in the yard to get enough soil to fill the bucket. Unfortunately it refused to stand up straight and I had to pile bricks around the trunk in the bucket to prop it up and hauled it inside the house.

When she saw it, Grace howled with laughter. When she was able to regain her self control she advised me it looked like "Charlie Brown's Christmas Tree" from the Peanuts cartoon Christmas Special.

I disagreed. I thought Charlie Brown's tree looked considerably better.

Anyway, this was our first Christmas tree and we have plenty of memories from it. One in particular, we had a long haired white cat Grace rescued from the laundromat that we named Honky Cat. She was cute and affectionate and she sat beside me as I strung popcorn onto a thread using a sewing needle to pierce each kernel. After a while I realized my garland was only a few feet long because Honky Cat was eating the popcorn as fast as I could string it. And after Christmas, I planted the hapless tree in the yard and it was dead in two weeks. Oops.

Seven years later we moved two blocks away to a much bigger house. This house had hardwood floors throughout, two fireplaces and THIRTEEN FOOT CEILINGS! I couldn't wait for December!

I had decided I had to have a Christmas tree to match the height of our ceilings so when the Christmas tree lots opened for business, we went to a nearby lot and spoke to the owner. I explained the situation and he said he had just the tree for us and led us to the largest Christmas tree I had ever seen. A church had ordered it but never came for it and he sold it to us for only $35. It was a monster. Tall, beautifully full with huge heavy limbs that could each hold a dozen ornaments which was good because my darling wife had bought hundreds of ornaments over the years. She is a Christmas junkie and most of them came from garage sales and flea markets and she intended to use every one.

But there were obstacles to overcome.

First of all the tree was extremely heavy. The burly tree lot owner helped me carry the tree to my truck and both of us were straining to haul it. That should have been a warning sign! I was rather muscular but even so that tree was a real strain to lift and drag from my truck when we arrived at our house. As luck would have it, none of our neighbors were available to lend me a hand moving the tree. Luckily our front door is nearly five feet wide and four inches thick. It is definitely the largest door I've ever seen that wasn't mounted on a medieval castle. If we are ever attacked by barbarians they will NOT get in through that door! But it was exactly what I needed to be able to drag that behemoth in. Still tied up, the limbs barely fit through the door. But as soon as I got it in I had to drag it out again because the trunk was also huge and our tree stand was not big enough to contain it. So I had to get a hatchet and whittle the trunk into a point that I could hammer the stand on. Balancing it to stand up straight was another chore but dedication got me through the task. Then I had to drag it back in and put it in place. However my wife could not decide where exactly that place was and I had to repeatedly move it, dodging a very large aquarium of fish, until she was happy. (The spot she decided on was where I had initially put it…)

And so we decorated our Christmas Sequoia that evening and it required nearly all of the decorations Grace had accumulated during our years together and we had a truly magnificent tree. When I say "We decorated the tree" it was actually ME! My darling wife was nearly 8 months pregnant with our future son and I did all the constant climbing up and down the 3 ladders I brought in. I hung up tens of thousands of lights and placed dozens and dozens of ornaments all the way to the top which usually required me leaning well beyond the safe zone in order to place a much valued ornament on the exact branch and precise spot my bulging wife requested (demanded) or to ensure the twinkling lights were properly spread out over the vertical mountain of greenery.

It was gorgeous. We were proud. I was exhausted.

Later we went to bed and our bedroom was on the other side of the living room wall. In fact we had a double fireplace, one side in the living room and one side in our bedroom, separated by a firewall that led to a single chimney. The fireplaces were huge half moon shaped and really produced heat and flame. We were snuggling in the bed basking in the glow of a fire and a door led into the living room and on the opposite wall in the living room hung a huge beveled mirror. The door was open and in the reflection of the mirror we marveled at the sight of our massive masterpiece of a Christmas tree. The lights were twinkling and flashing and reflecting on the myriad of decorations and it was truly beautiful.

Until we noticed the tree was slightly leaning. Then it was leaning at a much larger angle and then gravity took control and it was falling!

The tree crashed to the floor, barely missing the very large aquarium. With a shriek, I leapt up and rushed into the living room and waded deep into the branches and began to heave it back upright. Since I was wearing nary a stitch of clothing, the sharp needles gave me more reasons to shriek.

I started screaming for Grace to hurry in and help me but since she was eight months pregnant, her ability to hurry was extremely limited. I had her step into the tree between the branches and hold the tree vertically while I quickly threw on some clothes, grabbed the truck keys and sped to our other house which was only 2 blocks away. There I had some big concrete blocks stored in the backyard. I loaded a bunch up and zipped back home where my beloved mother-to-be was rapidly losing her love for this monstrous tree. I suspected she might also be losing her love for ME!

I quickly carried in the blocks and fortified the tree stand and built an impromptu wall around the trunk. Then I drove a couple of big nails into the wooden window frames on either side of the tree and tied fishing line from the tree trunk to the nails to help keep it upright.

At our annual Christmas party, everybody marveled at the beauty and magnificence of the tree. We received many compliments and a lot of photos were taken with most of our guests posturing in front of it. We smiled weakly at the remarks and wisely did not expound on the near disaster.

The tree survived through Christmas and New Years and since I dreaded the Herculean task of taking it down and repacking everything the tree stayed up through much of January even though my personal desire is to take our trees down before New Year's Eve. (In truth, if I had my "Scrooge-ish" desires met, the trees would be dismantled shortly after the last gift is opened. A divorce would likely happen before anybody sang the first verse of Auld Lang Syne. Grace's hopes are that I might forget to take down the trees and leave them up all year.) But daily massive amounts of needles piled up on the floor and our cat delighted in playing among them and spreading them throughout the house and so I began to take down and pack the decorations. Since Grace was very close to her due date she opted out from helping.

Well once the tree was denuded, I had the job of carefully lowering the tree to the floor to make sure our aquarium wasn't smashed, adding to the cleanup job I was already facing. Then I had to move most of the furniture so I could try and carry the tree out without dragging it, which would mess up the surface of our wooden floors. I have no idea how much that tree originally weighed but it certainly seemed to have gained weight during its final days, rather than losing any.

I managed to get it to our oversized front door where I learned that the tree which barely fit going in, was NOT going out. It seems that all of those limbs that had been tied up when it arrived, had now settled into their natural positions and refused to cooperate.

I got my lopping shears and tried removing limbs but these were very thick and quite strong and the lopping shears were ineffectual.

This left me with only one option.

If you've never cut up a tree in your living room with a chainsaw, you have missed one of life's most surreal experiences. The roar of the two stroke engine really resonates and echoes off the walls and will threaten to deafen you. But nothing can compete with the sound of a very pregnant woman howling with laughter from the back of the house. Grace laughed at me and my predicament until her sides hurt and her swollen belly shook like Saint Nick's belly was reported to have bounced.

Once I got the tree disassembled and stacked on the side of the road, I now faced a monumental cleanup. Needles, sap and more sawdust than I ever thought possible was spread to every point of the large room and a sizable portion somehow found its way to every room in the house, including the bathrooms. I was cleaning up sawdust for over six months.

The next day we found a Christmas Shop in a nearby city that was going out of business and had a 13 foot tall artificial tree they wanted desperately to dispose of and we got a bargain for the future Christmases. No more live trees.

We went through a series of Christmas trees over the years. Sometimes we had trees in every room. For a few years we had two tall slender trees in the living room and a small tree in the sunroom. The small one I decorated in a fishing motif. But gradually decorating for Christmas became less and less of a priority.

Then our son, Chad was admitted to Hillsong College in Sydney, Australia, to study Music Ministry. The college is an offshoot of Hillsong Church, a global mega-church with over 150,000 members in 23 countries. It is renowned for its use of music.

Chad was there for 3 years and for those years we simply took 4 day cruises at Christmas so we didn't have to decorate or cook and our house wasn't so empty. During those cruises I took a Santa Claus outfit which I wore on Christmas Eve on the ship. I let my white beard grow out and I was a great hit and many young and older ladies had their picture taken, perched on my lap.

HO! HO! HO!

And Christmas morning we always docked at Freeport in the Bahamas. I had a tee shirt that looked like Santa Claus' tunic and I wore a pair of red Bermuda shorts, a Santa hat and sandals. I looked like Santa on vacation and again I was stopped for many photos with ladies, many wearing bikinis. Life was good!

Freeport is a poor island and we tried to avoid some of the more disadvantaged areas. However one time we found ourselves in a neighborhood that did not look friendly and there was a gang of 6 to 7 tough looking youths bearing down on us. The biggest and meanest looking one stepped in front of me and growled, "Hey, Santa! What did you bring ME?" I didn't blink an eye as I replied, "NOTHING! I saw what you did with that goat!" He stepped back in shock and all of his buddies started hooting and laughing at him and saying things like "He saw what you did to a goat!" Suddenly he started smiling and chuckling himself and they stepped aside and let us continue on our way. Again, humor can defuse a potentially nasty situation.

Well we began putting up fewer and fewer decorations and the year we had Roscoe I had declared we would NOT put up a tree at all.

To my great surprise, Grace agreed. No tree.

And then she went behind my back and got a tree anyway. It was for Roscoe and I could not argue over it. She said she saw it on a MarkDown table for only $3. It was a tabletop tree about three feet tall and had a couple dozen lights on it. It was absolutely Cardinal sized and fit nicely on the coffee table. I got another string of small multi-colored lights that flashed on and off and added them to the tree. I then decorated it with some flashy sparkling bits of costume jewelry and made a string of paper clips and looped them around the limbs. I took a number of red and green plastic drinking straws and cut them into two or three inch pieces and fitted them over the ends of many of the limbs and put a full sized straw on the top branch. When we carried it into his room and placed it on the coffee table and plugged the lights in and turned them on, he was as excited as any young child would be upon seeing their first Christmas tree.

Grace and I sat on the couch and held hands as he flew around the room several times before landing on the coffee table and hopped excitedly around the base of the tree several times. Then he flew to the top of the tree and landed among the decorated limbs. He chewed on the string of paper clips and then several of the rings and bracelets before pulling about half of the straw pieces free and letting them fall to the table top or the floor. He would go to his seed bowl and select a sunflower seed and take it into the tree and crack the hull and remove the seed's meat and eat with gusto.

Occasionally he would come to us and sit on our knees or shoulders as if he wanted to thank us or share this marvellous gift with us.

To me it was the most memorable tree we've ever had.

As we moved towards Christmas we started to receive our annual Christmas cards from our friends. But we also started receiving cards from names I did not recognize and they were addressed: The Kirkpatricks AND ROSCOE. Some showed who really had the clout when they came as: ROSCOE and Family.

And some were simply addressed as: ROSCOE.

Sad to realize he got more cards than we did.

The 12 Days of Roscoe

During the days leading up to Christmas, I decided to create my own version of The 12 Days of Christmas with a Roscoe based perspective. Each day I posted on Facebook the epic with a new verse added until it ended up on Christmas Day: (sung to the tune THE 12 DAYS of CHRISTMAS)

On the twelfth day of Roscoe my true love gave to me

12 crickets singing

11 tweets tweeted

10 flowers eaten

9 messes to clean up

8 bowls of water

7 wax worms crawling

6 squirrels in a tree

5 pounds of seeeed!!!!!

4 blueberries

3 cats stalking

2 red feathers in my iced tea

And a Cardinal in the Christmas tree!!!!!!

Christmas, Cardinal Style

Christmas morning started as most mornings did. He greeted the coming sunrise with a string of insistent chirps until I opened his cage and he came to me for his waxworms before stretching his wings with a couple of circles around the room including banking off of the door and windows. He completed his breakfast with a cricket from the bin in the bottom of his cage. Our son, Chad, typically spends the night with us and when he rises we have a family breakfast together and then we open presents. When we were finished I went back into the sunroom with a couple of gifts for my other son. First I refilled his belly with a couple of waxworms and then I had two gifts for him. The first was a gift wrapped surprise. I held the small package in my lap and he hopped all around it examining the brightly colored paper and then he began to tear at the paper. This was the only time I let him do this and I was not sure how he would react but he seemed to relish the opportunity to "legally" tear something up. Inside was a plastic fishing worm from my tackle box and he grabbed the chartreuse colored string of slimy plastic and promptly flew away with it. I was carefully watching to make sure he had no opportunity to try and eat it and only moments later I held out a balled up piece of aluminum foil and he swooped back to me and traded items. He grasped it in his beak and flew to the floor where he rolled it back and forth, obviously not sure what to do with it. Then Grace brought in some warm water and I filled up his bathing bowl and put it on the shelf in his cage and he flew in and enjoyed his morning ritual. While he was distracted I removed the paper, worm and foil, fearing he might actually eat some of it.

Later I put up the best gift I received that Christmas. My son gave me a string of light up red Cardinals which I loved. I put them up in the sunroom framing the entrance doorway into our bedroom. Roscoe was very curious about them and perched above them peering down.

Will You Be My Friend?

Roscoe loved people. He enjoyed visitors and a number of people came to visit him. (Note: They came to visit the bird. Not me! It's hard to not feel envious of a few ounces of feathers and a beak.)

Kids especially loved seeing him and the thrill of feeding him was a special treat. However some of the younger kids were a bit of a concern. I worried that they would accidentally injure him in their enthusiasm so I would take special care with them. First I put Roscoe into his cage and closed all the doors. Then I would kneel down with them and open one of the middle doors and I would put a wax worm in their open palms and I would hold their arms at the wrist and guide their hands inside. Roscoe would land on their palms and take the morsel. Sometimes he would fly up into the perches and eat it but sometimes he stayed, perched on their hand or wrist to eat it. It always tickled them and they would giggle and wriggle with joy. And sometimes Roscoe would hop along their forearms towards them and I would hold them tightly so they didn't scare him or hurt him. Now they and their parents would laugh heartily because his tiny claws could really tickle tender skin. I'd be careful to block Roscoe from slipping out of the cage and he was always a good sport about it. He'd return to the perches and watch his visitors as they watched him. There were some good photos taken by the parents and often it was reported back to me that their kids talked about "feeding the red bird" for days and the children shared the photos and stories with their friends and Sunday School classes. Roscoe was a star!

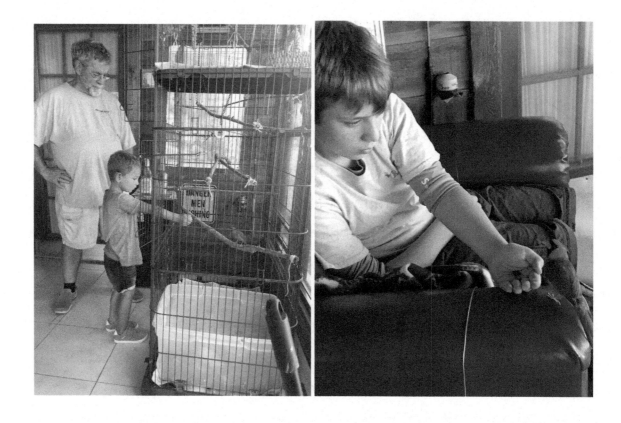

Adults also "flocked" to him. They would enter the sunroom and sit in the recliner or on the loveseat and offer him wax worms and he never refused them. It rarely took more than a minute before he would fly down from atop of his cage and land on the visitor's leg. He would cock his head to the side and gaze on them to make sure they were friendly. Then he'd hop to their open palm to receive their offerings. He almost always stayed after his snack and would move on the laps, shoulders or the top of heads. If the person was wearing jewelry he would pick at it with his beak and he was fond of gently pulling on mustaches and beards.

I have a medical issue that requires monthly infusions of antibodies and the infusions are done at our house by nurses. One of our nurses, Tonya, always demanded to visit him when we were done. Roscoe especially enjoyed her visits because she always had sparkly earrings and carried an ink pen in her breast pocket. Roscoe would fly to her and hover before her and steal her pens and try to fly away with them. He never could carry them far and it would slip from his beak and fall to the floor. He would land and try and drag it away before Tonya would retrieve it and return it to her pocket. He would fuss at her and again would try to commit petty larceny.

But not everybody was amused by the Krimson Kid! There were two people who were afraid of him. AND THESE TWO PEOPLE WERE THE BIGGEST INDIVIDUALS WHO MET HIM! (I will change the names and a few details to protect them and avoid their embarrassment!).

"Bill" was a policeman and stands about 6'4" and is built like a linebacker. I invited him to sit in the recliner and gave him a wax worm and when Roscoe landed and took the snack, "Bill" shrank back into the recliner apparently to gain what distance he could from the tiny bird. Roscoe ate the worm and then started hopping up "Bill's" considerable bulk. "Bill had a bushy bright red beard and I knew Roscoe wanted to check out the different colored bristles to see if any goodies might be there. "Bill" straightened up even more and I knew he was nervous and uncertain what to do so I walked over and shooed Roscoe away, but not before taking one of the funniest photos I've ever taken. "Bill's" eyes are wide open in terror as he stares at Roscoe as he sits on "Bill's" belly. I'm sure "Bill" has faced a number of possibly dangerous or threatening people in his law enforcement career without any concern but a 6 ounce Cardinal terrified him.

"Will" is an IT expert who came to our house to hook up Google Home for us. I know him slightly through a civic group I joined and he supports the group's computer needs. "Will" is another large man who appears to be capable of easily defending himself should the need arise.

Now to be fair, "Will" did not know what he was about to face. Roscoe was on his highest perch in the room and unless you knew to look there, he was almost invisible. I wanted to surprise "Will" and so gave him no warning of what was about to happen. I honestly thought he would be delighted by the experience because he was always a friendly jolly fellow and stupidly I assumed a bird landing on him would bring him joy.

Boy, was I wrong!

I told him to hold out his hand and he did, but when I dropped the wax worm in his very large palm, a look of disgust and revulsion came on his face and he immediately flung it to the floor. I picked it up and told him it was just a simple grub and had no teeth or stinger and could not harm him in any way. I held it in front of him but he was on the verge of freaking out. I explained nothing would hurt him and he would enjoy what was about to happen but he would need to let the worm sit in his palm for a few seconds.

I did not know he is a germaphobe and the idea of an insect touching his skin was extremely repulsive to him. Had I known I would have never done what I was doing. I may be thoughtless but I'm rarely cruel. Especially to people much larger than me!

It must have been a real test of faith but he slowly opened his massive hand and I dropped the tiny plump pupae onto his flesh. Roscoe must have been watching all of this unfold because almost immediately he swooped down and landed on "Will's" arm to take his treat. "Will" screamed in terror and jumped up and fled from the room after again flinging the wax worm away from him. Roscoe flew back to his perch, no doubt confused at this turn of events. Nobody had ever reacted to him like this before. I snatched up the fallen worm from the floor and dropped it inside his cage. He quickly found it and ate it. I followed the upset IT man into the living room where he was snatching up his tools intending to vacate our house as soon as possible. I managed to calm him down and apologized several times, explaining it was just a small bird and that I had meant no harm. With much begging I convinced him to step to the door leading to the sunroom and peek through the windows. Once he realized what had happened, he relaxed enough to complete the job for me. However I noticed he charged me considerably more than he had originally quoted!

All Good Things Come to an End

(Lesson: Keep Your Mouth Shut!)

January was uneventful and our lives settled into a routine. Roscoe grew a bit more and his coloring became a deep beautiful red.

And then January 31, 2019 happened.

The Super Bowl was a few days away and if you are a football fan or not, there was excitement in the air.

I received a call on my cell phone but since I was in nasty traffic and did not recognize the number, I let it roll into voicemail and promptly forgot about it. Later I remembered and when I listened to it it was a man, identifying himself as an investigator with the Florida Wildlife Commission and he said it was critically important that I call him back. Now during the Thanksgiving and Christmas holiday season I received a number of calls from people claiming to represent The Police Benevolent Society, various Firemens' Associations, Military Aid and others. I know that many are fake or those people who actually do work for companies that "help" worthy causes work for companies that take nearly all of the donations with very little going to the charities. I used to work with people who were part-time solicitors for these groups and they reported tremendous pressure to squeeze donations mostly from people who could least afford to give. They said their bosses all drove really nice cars.

I have always tried to help people in need but I must confess the large number of panhandlers I have been exposed to in recent years make me hesitant or unwilling to pass over my hard earned money.Once a woman approached me at an intersection asking for money. I noticed her jewelry, designer jeans and well manicured fingernails. I rolled down my window and pulled out my wallet and innocently asked if she could break a $50 bill. She assured me she could and pulled out a huge wad of cash and started peeling off $20, $10s and $5s before getting to the singles. I looked her in the eye and remarked that if she could break a $50 then she didn't need MY money and rolled the window up. Her comments were very unladylike.

Another time we were in Atlanta for a business conference just before Christmas. My company put us up at the Ritz Carlton downtown and we were 3 blocks from a Florsheim shoe store. I wore a difficult to find size of dress shoe and only Florsheim had a shoe that comfortably fit me. I called to learn they had 3 pairs in my size in stock so we walked down to the store. All along the route people were begging for money and I would rather give to 9 who don't need it than miss 1 who did, so I had a bunch of $1 bills which I handed out like Halloween candy.

Then we saw the man in the wheelchair.

It was bitterly cold and he was shivering like crazy. His wheelchair was pulled into an alcove to get a little shelter from the wind and he looked so miserable I gave him nearly all of my money. Then we went to the shoe store.

Marge, the store manager, was measuring my feet when I heard the door open. I looked up to see the crippled man WALK inside PUSHING HIS WHEELCHAIR! Then the following conversation took place between Marge and the "crippled panhandler".

Man: "Hi Marge!"

Marge: "Hey Bill! How's it going out there?"

Bill: "@#%%^& *#%$! Some #$&^* is in MY space! I've barely made $100 this morning! And I'm freezing my ass off! I'm going to get some coffee!" and then he walked into the back of the store into the storage area. A minute later he emerges sipping hot coffee and yells out, "I need to make a phone call!"

Marge yells back, "You know where the phone is!" Then the beggar walks behind the counter and picks up the store phone and dials it.

Apparently he didn't recognize me even though I am only a few feet away. All I could think about was how much cash I had given him but eventually begrudgingly came to admire his style.

But I still can't believe his relationship to the shoe store and its manager. It seems this behavior was accepted as a normal part of street life.

So I generally ignore these types of calls and instead Grace and I regularly donate to a selected group of charities that we know will use our money as we intended. Therefore, I did not call the gentleman back.

However, later, something about the message started to bother me. Maybe, just maybe it was legitimate.

So the next day I called the man back and he thanked me profusely. Then he told me that somebody had filed a complaint against me because I had an imprisoned Cardinal. He asked if it was true.

All kinds of thoughts and answers ran through my head. The bird was dead, had escaped or to simply deny the existence of Roscoe. A myriad of excuses, tall tales and simple lies presented themselves to me. But since I felt I had done nothing wrong, I simply confessed. "Yes there is a Cardinal that lives in our sunroom." I gave him a quick summary: he was days old when we found him, raised and trained him and released him over and over but the bird obviously wanted to live with us and he was living the spoiled life of a Royal Prince.

Then he shattered my world and told me he was going to have to confiscate my little buddy and release him in a wildlife management area.

If you are unfamiliar with the term wildlife management area it is not like a zoo where the birds and animals are cared for. No, this is merely a patch of woods where hunting is not allowed. But there is a subclass of human hunters, who see these areas as spots where there are likely more animals to kill than normal since law abiding people won't go there.

If you are ever in one you will notice that all of the NO HUNTING and NO TRESPASSING signs are riddled by bullets. The resident 4 legged animals did not shoot these signs. Two legged animals did.

Plus all of the predators live there. Remember the close calls Roscoe had with the hawk, snake and cat? This would NOT be a friendly abode.

Plus it's February. WINTER! Few leaves on the trees and his red feathers will make him a beacon, advertising a tasty morsel. And it's cold, rainy and very windy. Food will be scarce. Shelter will be hard to find.

A Probable Death Sentence.

Dear God, no!

I was driving down the road when this bomb exploded in my lap and I was stunned and in shock. I could literally feel my blood pressure soaring upward rapidly and my head began pounding. I couldn't speak. I couldn't think. I was barely driving safely.

I told the officer I had to get off of the phone and he tried to convince me to stay on. Doubtless he feared ever getting me back on and then facing the task of more drastic measures to acquire Roscoe. I stammered that I feared I was about to have a stroke and had to get off of the phone. I promised I would call back but he still pressured me to stay on the phone. I knew he was hoping to take Roscoe immediately and I was desperate to avoid that. Finally I simply hung up.

I immediately called my wife and told her. She was horrified and we discussed options and possibilities but already in my heart I knew my time with my Feathered Friend was coming to an end.

I called the officer back the following day as I had promised and he was grateful that I had. I doubt many people are as cooperative.

I again explained the situation. Yes, I had raised him but had released him so many times. I told him I had photographs and videos of his releases and of him obviously being free. I argued about his chances of survival and I pointed out that Cardinals are not truly migratory and so the Migratory Bird Act truly did not apply.

He listened patiently. He was sympathetic and empathetic but he stuck to his guns. Roscoe must be turned over to him to be released.

But he did grant me a temporary reprieve. It was a Thursday and he agreed to delay taking my buddy until Monday morning, giving me a few more days with him.

I tried to come to terms with the situation. I told myself that he still was a wild creature and deserved his chance to live the life he was supposed to live. I tried to convince myself that I had prepared him to fend for himself and he could find the foods he should eat. I thought over and over that even though he had spacious and comfortable living quarters, it was nothing to the endless horizons of being outside.

And then I would remember the snake, the hawk and the cat and the countless dangers he would be exposed to. I thought about the winter winds and freezing temperatures, the summer heat, the pounding thunderstorms and even hurricanes and how could he endure them? Where would he sleep? How would he know where the safe spots were? I remembered how the other birds attacked him to drive him away. And most of all, I thought about the loneliness and fear he would have and the confusion over having the only life he knew turned upside down.

I wondered if he would miss me? Or even remember me?

I wept and I prayed.

I went home and went into his room. I sat on the couch and he stayed primarily in his cage. The cage where he was perfectly safe. I talked to him and tried to explain that a wonderful opportunity was coming for him soon and he needed to remember all of the things he had learned. I hoped he would leave the cage and come to me. I wanted to feel him on top of my head, pulling at my hair. Or hopping along my shoulder, tweaking my ears. But he remained aloof.

I posted on FaceBook on the various sites where I had shared the stories of his exploits. I explained what was coming because there were so many people who adored him and the stories. I didn't place blame. I didn't challenge. I didn't curse or denigrate. Just an honest explanation of what was likely to take place.

I had a terrible night. The little sleep I got was filled with bad dreams involving Roscoe. It was horrible.

Facing the Music

The next morning I opened up FaceBook and was shocked by the massive response I received from my posts. People were outraged, sad and sympathetic at the possible loss of Roscoe. Of course there were a few negative comments like "He deserves to be free!" or "You should never have interfered!". I basically ignored those people. Generally a good handful of people would respond and defend me and my actions, but this time the support was surprisingly and overwhelmingly in my corner. That was reassuring.

But I was shocked by the willingness of some people to get involved. People announced they wanted to collect and donate cash presumably for possible legal fees and / or fines. There were people who wanted to contact the local tv networks to drum up support for me. Sort of a feathered FREE WILLY movement. People wanted to contact attorneys and local officials. People were willing to make signs and drive to our house to picket and prevent the officer from being able to gain access to our property.

But most of all there were a number of people willing to come and spirit Roscoe away and hide him until the coast was clear. One woman was willing to drive from Macon, Georgia, a distance of around 270 miles.

Sort of an avian Underground Railroad.

It was shocking, it was wonderful, it was heartfelt. And I had to shoot everybody down. This misguided generosity could not result in a happy ending. I was fighting the Federal Government on this one. I was violating The Federal Migratory Bird Act. I could be slapped with fines of up to $15,000 and 5 years in prison.

My son said it best. "Dad, you're too old to go to prison". With my arthritis I'd probably keep dropping the soap in the showers. I have watched OZ, the HBO series on prison life and I knew at least 3 ways to make a shiv for protection but wanted to avoid the effort if possible.

Actually I doubt they send birdnappers to Federal prison but I have heard of people getting $1000 fines for possession of a single hawk's feather. I wonder what the going rate for a complete Cardinal would cost me. Too damn much, I'm sure.

But the real reason I had basically conceded was I'm too much of a law and order kind of guy. Early on, somebody warned me of the possible consequences I might face. I researched what they told me and found it was true. I also remembered vividly my brother, Mike, had with the otter he raised. He had only the best intentions for Ozzie and gave him superb care but he still nearly went to jail over his love for the otter. I had given Roscoe his chances at freedom but he didn't seem to appreciate the effort and I had hoped that it would give me an excuse, a rationalization, a GET OUT OF JAIL FREE card, but apparently it did not.

I received some correspondence from one of his many friends. She is the wife of one of our State Senators and she had approached her husband about the situation. He then assigned one of his staff people to make some contacts within the State's officials to see if anything could be done. Unfortunately it was Super Bowl Weekend and it was difficult to contact people. But I so very much appreciated the offer and the effort. I instinctively knew there was little chance of a Reprieve From The Governor.

If only her husband WAS the Governor...

Sunday afternoon, I sat on the couch in the sunroom, savoring our last few hours together. I felt like Roscoe knew something was going on because he was especially attentive to me. He would come to me and sit on my head or shoulders, lap or knee and hop back and forth checking me out. He would cock his head and gaze at me and then gently pull on my hair or earlobe or the buttons on my shirt. I whispered softly to him, reassuring him that he would be fine and telling him how much we loved him. I tried very hard to be happy that he would soon have the freedom I always wanted for him, but then I would wonder how he was going to stay warm in the cold, dry in the rain, and safe from all of the many creatures that would want to eat him.

He even allowed me to gently pet and stroke him. He wasn't really fond of being petted but he tolerated it for an amazingly long time.

Happily I managed to video much of this time and I cherish rewatching it.

The sun was setting and it was time for him to settle down and sleep. For the last time I watched him fly into his cage and pick the perch he wanted to sleep on. I slowly closed the cage doors and whispered goodnight to him and turned off the lights. It was one of the lowest points of my life.

I awoke at 3:00am and got a flashlight. I quietly crept into his room and opened the doors to his cage. I turned on the flashlight and aimed it on him and swiftly grabbed him with my hand and removed him and placed him in the cat carrier. It no doubt frightened him and he was rapidly beating his wings as I left the room. But I didn't want to try and capture him in the morning, I knew it would be a challenge and probably traumatic for him. I did not want his last morning with us to be more unsettling for him than necessary.

As the sun began to rise he started becoming active. I could hear him hopping back and forth and he started calling to me to release and feed him. Instead I dressed and went outside. It was a chilly morning and again I worried about him contending with the weather. However the bird activity in the yard reminded me that God does provide for all living creatures and my spirits raised slightly. After all, these birds had survived just fine.

At 7:30, a truck pulled into our driveway. There is an automatic gate and it could just barely get off of the street. Inside I saw a burly young man wearing a uniform. He waved at me and I gave him a half hearted wave back. I entered the house and told Grace that the officer was here and I picked up the cat carrier with its little prisoner and headed to the door. Grace followed.

Confession and Apology

Ok, I owe my loyal Facebook readers a confession and apology and at this point, I'd like to clear the air.

I lied.

I try very hard to be an honest person. I really do. As a storyteller I occasionally apply a touch of what is commonly referred to as "poetic license". It's mainly to make a funny story a bit more comedic or to build up a dramatic situation, but this was much more. But I promised at the beginning of this book that it was a true story and now I'm going to confess and apologize.

I led people to believe that Roscoe was hauled away to an unknown spot and then kicked out to fend for himself. That WAS the officer's intentions but I pleaded for a change in venue. I promised I would cooperate fully, IF Roscoe was released here, on our property. Since I think the officer could tell how stressed I was and when I explained why, he accepted my proposal.

As I stated earlier, our little piece of earth is a bird's paradise. There are plenty of trees and bushes where the birds can safely nest, hide or rest. There is a massive amount of natural food along with a very healthy distribution of sunflower seed available from nearly a dozen feeders. There is a natural brackish water tidal creek, miles of marsh and several birdbaths and watering spots. One has a misting station where the birds can frolic in a cloud of cool water to ward off the summer heat.

We have a very long driveway and I headed towards the truck. When I was about 30 feet away, I stopped, put the carrier on a small table and opened the door of the carrier. In all honesty, I wasn't sure the officer would fully keep his end of the bargain. I could imagine him snatching my little friend and stuffing him into a box or cage and speeding away. So this was my way of making sure that did not happen.

There was a flash of red and my little friend zipped out, up and away.

He flew at breakneck speed out of our yard, across the neighbor's property and into the woods that make up much of the next neighbor's property and disappeared. Before he had always flown up into a nearby tree but this time he made a mad streak away from the confines of the cat carrier. And away from me. He was gone. Gone.

Aftermath

The officer was now standing outside of his truck scribbling madly on a clipboard. When he finished he approached the gate and I went there too. He shook my hand and then admonished me for not checking his identification first, then he handed me the clipboard and a pen and instructed me to sign the warning citation I was receiving, before handing me a copy. He then thanked me for cooperating, shook my hand again and then got back in his truck and departed.

There was no sign of Roscoe.

Yes, I called him. I whistled for him. I hauled his cage out and placed it in clear view and loaded it with food. I put a couple of security cameras in place around the cage and we got a few quick glimpses of a male Cardinal in the cage but it always vanished within seconds.

I don't know what I would have done, had he returned willingly to us. Probably I would have snatched him and run into the house. I won't lie, I desperately wanted him back with us but I also realized God had probably forced me to do the right thing.

When God speaks, you better listen!

Likewise when The Government speaks. It speaks loudly AND carries a big stick.

Later that afternoon, I received a surprising telephone call. It was from Eric Sutton, who identified himself as being the Head of the Florida Wildlife Commission. He was calling me to personally apologize for the way my case was handled.He said he had been notified of the situation but did not realize his officer was pursuing it so rapidly and unaware that Roscoe had already been released already. He told me that he had been investigating "other solutions" when he learned that it was too late. I was touched that he made the effort to call me. He asked that I "not hate" his organization and I assured him I did not, that I understood that the laws are the laws but that I felt there should be exceptions since the bird obviously wanted to remain in our care. He confessed that the Federal Migratory Bird Act is a flawed piece of legislation, but is still the law. I told him that while growing up, my dream job would have been to be a Wildlife Officer.

He asked me if there was anything he could do for me and I confessed there was. I wanted to read the complaint filed against me to see what the complainant had stated. He told me he could not provide the person's name and I assured him that was not what I wanted. I simply wanted to know why the person had felt compelled to report me. Was it in the interest of protecting the bird or a personal attack intended to hurt me and maybe have me arrested. He promised me he would make sure I got a copy of the complaint but I never got it and finally gave up. I only hope it was for the right reasons.

For the next several days I looked frantically for some sign of him, some tiny assurance that he was ok and doing well. But there was nothing. I put out cameras and once for just a second there was a glimpse of a Cardinal on it. Then nothing.

After a few days I tore down the cage, cleaned it and stored it. I boxed up all of his "toys" and his feeding and bathing bowls. I scrubbed down the sunroom and again the cats were allowed to enter it. It was as if he had never been a part of our lives. I watched many of the videos I had made of him and reviewed the album of photos. I reread the Facebook posts I had written and the hundreds of replies and comments that had been written. I erased some of them. But most of them, I kept.

I never stepped outside without looking for a sign of him or a snippet of his songs and chirps. I bought several sets of expensive binoculars and placed them in strategic spots in the house and yard. I spent hours scanning the trees for a flash of red.

I began to see a large red male Cardinal in the yard more often than before. I would stop and talk to it and call his name. My vision is weak and, well frankly, one Cardinal looks like another, but Grace and I were always sure it was him. He would look carefully at me, cock his head and look as if he was preparing to fly to me. When he did this, my heart would race and EVERY TIME as it appeared he was coming to me, a female Cardinal would fly past right in front of him and he would race after her. <u>Every</u> time.

That's my boy all right.

I believe God, obviously, had a hand in that.

I would smile wistfully and turn away, knowing it was all somehow working out as it should. I hated it but I knew it was as it should be.

And we have suddenly become very popular with the Cardinal crowd. We now have more in our yard than I could ever imagine. Males and females crowd our feeders. I have added a pair of suet feeders that are especially well used. I had put out suet in the past and it generally dried up to a hard chunk of dried fat and seeds which I tossed away. Now I replace them about every few days. I have to buy sunflower seed every time Tractor Supply has it on sale and I stock up. In addition to the Cardinals, Chickadees, Finches, Sparrows, Doves, Mockingbirds, Blue Birds and other species are constant visitors. Even a pair of Blue Jays, which we've never seen here before, have joined the crowd.

Many many years ago we bought a Norman Rockwell print at an auction. It just appealed to us and has hung in our bedroom ever since. It shows a man playing a flute in front of a huge aviary that is filled with many species of birds. Because of the plethora of birds that we enjoy in our own yard, we often feel like we are now living in that painting. In the center of the picture is a Cardinal and it appears the Cardinal is listening to the man's music.

I wish I could play the flute.

The Final Goodbye

One morning, just before sending this book to the publisher, as I do daily, I arose as the sun was beginning to cross the horizon. I fed the cats before going outside to tend to the chickens. I always take a couple of slices of bread with me and after opening the coop they will mill around my feet for a snack of a morsel of bread. They all take their treat from my fingers and then some run to be first in their favorite nesting boxes and some sprint to get to the chicken feed I have spread and the rest stay behind to finish off the remaining bread. Once my hand was empty I shooed them away and took the hose and washed out the coop.

As I was doing that I heard birdsong coming from all over the yard. They are particularly vocal at this time of the morning and I heard the chirps of several Cardinals mixed in with the songs of Mockingbirds, Woodpeckers, Sparrows, Finches and Chickadees. High overhead a hawk was screaming and squirrels were chattering in the pecan trees. There were a couple of Cardinals high in a tree in front of me and another in the Crepe Myrtles by the street. And one behind me.

They all soon wandered off seeking breakfast but the one behind me continued to chirp insistently and then it became louder as if it wanted my attention. Slowly I turned to face the sound and by the fence in an Althea bush sat a male Cardinal. A big beautiful boy, with feathers so red and bold he was truly magnificent. He seemed to be trying to communicate with me so I stood and watched and listened. He sang a series of notes and seemed to be singing directly to me. Then I began to softly sing back to him. I sang all of the silly morning songs I used to sing to Roscoe and he cocked his head at the tunes as if he recognized them and I also did all of the whistles and clicks I used with Roscoe.

Normally after a short concert of my repertoire the birds would fly away but this one did not. He watched me intently and then began to travel up and down the limbs of the Althea. He'd go down to the ground and then back up. He never stopped watching me and after I stopped my chatter, he continued his. He gave me a long chain of chirps that slightly varied in tone and volume. It was as if he was bringing me up to date on his life. Maybe he was telling me about raising a brood of his own offspring. Maybe it was how much he appreciated the sunflower seed I left in the feeders. Maybe it was about how delightful it was to fly wherever he wanted, without limits. I responded by telling him how much I missed him and loved him and what a challenge and what a joy he had been.

And I remembered. I remembered holding that tiny ball of feathered life. I recalled the feelings of anguish and unfairness that it's life depended solely on me. I remembered the overwhelming agony of feeling useless and impotent for being unable to feed him and save his life. And then I remembered the joy, pride and wonderment as bit by bit, I learned what to do and he rallied, recovered and finally began to thrive and grow. I was a firsthand witness to the miracle that was him.

And I was humbled to have played a part in that miracle.

After at least 5 minutes of this a female flew into the Althea just below him. It was at this point that my previous "conversations" had always ended with the female (we dubbed her "Roscolina") flying away with the male in hot pursuit. But this time after a short stay, she flew away and he stayed and continued to "talk" to me.

I slowly took a couple of steps towards him until we were about 20 feet apart. He tensed up as if preparing to take wing but when I stopped advancing, he relaxed.

We continued our "conversation". I told him if he ever wished to come home again he would be welcome and Roscolina could also come. I promised I would buy him anything and everything he could want. Fat wax worms, the biggest crickets, fresh flowers and seed and fruit would be on his menu. I would festoon the sunroom with toys and shiny objects of all kinds and sizes. He would live like a king.

As I was prattling on about this I was also nervously wondering what would I do if he actually came to me and allowed me to capture him? I would be overjoyed but I'd also know I was making a monstrous mistake.

Yes, I wanted him back in the sunroom where I could play with him, care for him and love him. Visitors, and especially children, could again experience the joy of feeding a live Cardinal from their fingers and then laugh as his tiny claws tickled them as he hopped on their body. I missed that so much. I especially missed how he could sense when I was about to leave "his" room and so would fly and land on my shoulder or atop of my head to prevent me from going. It always worked too. I would stay and enjoy his close presence until being dismissed when he flew away. There was never a doubt as to who was in command.

But I also knew that the sunroom was no longer his world. THIS, the outdoors, was his world, his kingdom, his 'hood. This is what he was created to be and where he truly belonged. And as much as I loved and adored him, I could never replace the other Cardinals of his flock.

Besides, while Cardinals only live a couple of years in the wild they can easily live 20 years or more in captivity. And I probably won't live that long. My joints protest when I stoop and bend and it would become harder and harder to properly clean his cage and the sunroom. It wouldn't be fair to put this on somebody else and down the road someone may decide to open the door to the backyard and send him out. Now older himself he may have his own issues in regards to flying and finding food. He may have lost his survival skills and become an easy prey.

I shook my head. He can not come back.

Our time together had come to an end.

We continued to talk to each other. Minutes passed and this was easily the longest time one of the Cardinals had stayed so close to me. Several times he looked like he was about to fly to me but he didn't.

I was smiling as I admired what a beautiful bird this one was. I prayed fervently that this truly was Roscoe and he was still here   and still alive and healthy. I was finally at peace with the outcome of my experiences with him. Even if this was an imposter, I had done my best and I had enjoyed a most unique experience that few have. My earlier mistakes and ignorance with Jay and Dave had maybe been balanced out.

It had been nearly 15 minutes and I knew Grace was waiting for me so we could eat breakfast. My legs were getting a bit tired and I could not stand there much longer. I looked at him and he looked at me and then he flew straight into the blueberry thicket. This was where I always recovered him after he had been released. Was this another sign?

Slowly I walked over to the spot where he had disappeared into the bushes. I was fearful he was waiting there for me to cup him in my hands as I had done those times before and bring him back to the sunroom and the cage that had been his home. In addition to the blueberries a massive azalea exists there. I peered into the blueberry plants and then carefully circled the azalea and the rest of the thicket but there was no sign of any red bird. I would have likely seen him if he flew out of the back of the bushes or up into the branches of the nearby trees and had not.

I was alone.

Had I been hallucinating or dreaming? Was the bird a figment of my imagination? A feathered ghost?

The yard was strangely silent. No birds singing, no squirrels chattering. Even Bob, our extremely vocal rooster, was quiet.

I walked down the driveway and picked up our newspaper and as I headed to the house I searched the trees for a speck of red. There was none. I went inside and closed the door.

God has been very good to me. Maybe I have been blessed because I care about other creatures or maybe I care about other creatures because I have been blessed. Either way, it's been good.

Thank you, God.

Part II

As I stated earlier, before I could finish this project, another bird briefly came into our lives and because of the similarities with this little fellow to the beginning of our time with Roscoe, I felt compelled to include that story into the book. And then Grace reminded me of our first bird (that did not die on me) and she insisted I include a brief synopsis of what happened with him.

This book was nearly titled THREE BIRDS IN THE ROAD. You'll soon understand why.

And so let me introduce you to Jack and Fred. (There is no extra charge, so relax and enjoy!)

Jack

History repeats itself. So does life. We make the same mistakes over and over. We follow the same paths. I wonder if the fates are playing with us?

Recently we were driving home and had stopped at the last stop sign before our destination. Grace was driving and she waited for two cars that were approaching to make their left hand turns in front of us before making our left turn on the way to our favorite little patch of Earth.

I was reminiscing. We had found Roscoe a short distance from where we were waiting and I often recall the chain of events that led to our meeting. He was in the middle of the road, hopping around trying to escape the heat from the road that was burning his feet.

It was then that I saw the silhouette of what appeared to be a very small bird. It was also in the road, in the left lane, and in the direct path of the first car as it made its turn. I expected it to fly or hop away as the car bore down on it but watched in horror as the first car made its turn and it's right side tires missed the bird by only a couple of inches.

The bird made no move to escape. It did not fly nor hop away from the huge metal monster that had just barely missed it.

Then the second car made its turn and again the bird did not flee. This car literally rolled over the bird and I had the sickening realization it had certainly crushed the feathered creature. But when the car passed it was still there. Somehow the tires had missed it, but only by maybe an inch or so.

Something was amiss. Perhaps it wasn't really a bird but something that resembled one. A stick or a pine cone. I had to know.

I got out of the car.

I walked up to it and saw it was indeed a tiny sparrow. I knelt down and it made no move to avoid me. I picked it up and it struggled for a few seconds before calming down. I carried it off of the road towards the roadside trees where I opened my hand for it to fly away.

It did not move.

I prodded it with my finger and instead of escaping it climbed up on my finger and quietly perched there.

I returned to our car with my passenger firmly attached to my digit. He stayed there during the drive home and when I entered our house. I carried him into the sunroom.

Grace brought in Roscoe's little basket and placed it on the stone coffee table. I moved him onto it. I left our tiny visitor in Grace's care as I went to our garage and again retrieved one of our cat carriers. I washed it out and again made a number of perches that fit between the ventilation slits on the side. I carried it into our sunroom and Grace was sitting on our loveseat and the tiny feathered fellow was calmly sitting beside her.

Since it was a sparrow, I named it Jack. Jack Sparrow. For the main character in the Disney movie, PIRATES OF THE CARIBBEAN. It was then we saw he appeared to be blind or maybe missing its eyes. He was so small it was hard to really tell. A little research said it might be conjugavitis and may spread to both eyes and cause permanent blindness. Possible treatments included washing the eyes with saline.

We then drove to the nearby Winn Dixie grocery store and asked the pharmacist for some various sized syringes and when she learned the purpose she gladly gave us a good variety and pointed out the saline.

Back at the house I opened a can of cat food and drained out some of the gravy into a small bowl. I added a couple of meat shreds and chopped it as finely as possible. I added enough water so it could be drawn into a syringe and easily expelled from it. These were the lessons I had learned from the first days of caring for Roscoe. I had no way of knowing if the tiny ball of feathers was an infant or fully grown. And it could not see any food presented to it so I'd have to feed it myself and this was the only concoction I knew to fix. It had kept Roscoe alive when he first came to us. Maybe it could work again.

While I was preparing Jack's repast, Grace brought in some cotton balls and soaked them in the saline solution and some cotton balls also were soaked with fresh water. Then I held him gently in my hand as Grace carefully wiped off his eyes. She did it several times while wiping with fresh water between the saline applications. He did not struggle nor object. We looked at where his eyes would be and saw no evidence that eyes were there. We realized why he had not tried to escape the cars that nearly ended his life. He was totally blind. I could only imagine the terror he had experienced as the roar of the car approached and then passed by. So sad.

Then I took over and tried to feed him. I was using the largest syringe we had received, thinking the liquid would flow easily and some of the small food particles would pass into his beak and down his throat. But it did not work. He resisted my efforts to force the syringe into his beak and the liquid flowed down his beak and onto his chest.

He wasn't happy. Neither was I. It brought back the unhappy memories of trying and mostly failing to feed that little Cardinal.

After several futile attempts, Grace took the smallest syringe and pulled the liquid into it. Then she offered it to him on the side of his beak and with a minimum of pressure he opened his beak and eagerly accepted her offerings. Success!

She gave him 3 syringes full of the liquid and I decided to call it quits for a while. He seemed tired and confused about what was happening. We put him on the handle of the basket and put it in a cardboard box and left him alone. But before I released him, he expressed his gratitude for our efforts by crapping in my hand. A card or gift certificate would have been a more meaningful thank you.

NOTE: If you recall during the story of Roscoe, when we were first trying to learn what we needed to do to try and save his life, I contacted a very well known bird rescue organization near here. This same place, my brother had done a tremendous amount of volunteer work for and I had hauled fresh fish to them to feed their predatory birds. I reported I left numerous messages for them telling them I needed some information and mentioning my brother and my efforts for them and it was ten days before I heard back from them. In fact, I called every organization I could find within a 150 mile radius and only received a response from an animal rescue after more than a week. (I believe they contacted the first group and coerced them into finally calling me back). Well I had the same response from them again. I left a message asking how to treat my tiny sparrow and they have never called. I also called a local bird hospital who would only help me if I paid them. They did give me a third group to call and they also did not return my call.

The first group had been included in our wills. Grace and I wanted to express our support to a number of local and national groups whose works and efforts we believed in. I appreciated what this group was trying to do and assigned them a very generous stipend upon my demise.

Not anymore! After being ignored again, Grace and I made an appointment with our attorney and had them removed from our wills. We picked a different charity to benefit from our passings.

I have often wished that Hallmark made a "Screw You!" greeting card. I would have ordered a case of them and this organization would have received the first one.

Every hour and a half we went back in and repeated the saline baths and fed him. He was still listless but did not seem to panic or be afraid. He allowed us to handle him by either holding him in my hand or perched on a finger. As the sun was setting we treated and fed him again and left him alone for the evening.

Each time we fed him, he placed another watery token of his gratitude in my hand. Love means never having to say I'm sorry.

The next morning he was still alive but still lethargic. He did not resist when I picked him up nor when we fed him the same solution as before. He did accept several doses of the liquid and we treated both eyes several times and he did not object but both eyes were still slammed shut and we could not tell if he actually had eyes. I began to have a bad feeling about this situation.

He received two more feedings and eye treatments that morning and when I went to care for him that afternoon one of his eyes was open and apparently functioning. In fact he made an aborted attempt to escape by flying into the nearby windows. Happily he mostly fluttered to them and so when he hit them it did no damage to the bird or our house.

Now when I placed him back in the cat carrier, perched on the handle of the little basket, I added a shallow bowl of water and some dried mealworms, chicken feed crumbles and cracked corn and left him alone.

During the day I fed him several syringes of liquid and then after what had become the standard anointing of my palm, returned him to the cat carrier. But now he went up into the perches of limbs I had made for him, meaning his eyes were functioning well enough to leave the basket and go higher. But I had no idea if he was eating the solid foods I placed in the box.

Later I went to check on him and now both eyes were open! However one of them had a red ring around it and we guessed it was showing his eyes were improved but not healed. Now it looked like he had been in the snacks I provided but I still gave him the liquid grub. But I noticed he wasn't as willing to accept it as before and I hoped it meant he had a full belly. He again tried to escape and flew into the window but with more strength than before. Things were looking up. Literally.

He continued to crap in my hand. At least I knew his digestive system was functional. I hoped they weren't acts of vengeance or anger.

The next morning both eyes were still open but the red ring was still evident. He managed to escape twice while trying to feed and treat him and he definitely was stronger than before. His digestive tract was also continuing to work as another fecal offering was given.

Now I had a dilemma to face. He wasn't 100% healed with the eyes but he was on the way to better health. But I was not sure what, if any, solid food he was actually consuming since we never saw him eating. Birds have a rapid metabolism and must consume calories continuously or starve to death. Would he be better off kept in captivity until the red ring disappeared or should we release him immediately so he could hopefully continue his natural diet. If we didn't release him he may easily starve to death as the liquid diet was certainly not enough to sustain him. But released too soon, if his eyes worsened again, he would be in real danger.

Well, Mother Nature made our decision for us as it immediately started to storm. Hard winds and rains battered the landscape and we would not release him into that.

The rains continued for the entire morning and into early afternoon and we continued to treat and feed him and he continued to soil my palm.

Apparently a tradition had begun.

Around 1:30pm, the rain and wind abated and the sun came out. Birds began to sing and fly around our yard and visit our feeders. The weatherman predicted no more rains and I made a decision. I captured him one last time and we fed him and gave his eyes a final treatment. The red ring remained but both eyes were open and bright. He also was struggling to escape my grasp which I took as a good sign.

We lured our cats inside with food and a healthy dose of fresh catnip and then Grace, Jack and I snuck out the front door.

We walked down the driveway to the midpoint of our property. There are a dozen large trees, plenty of bushes and shrubs and four feeders with sunflower seeds and two suet feeders. A couple of bird baths complete the accommodations.

Grace snapped a few final photos and I opened my hand. Jack stood on my open palm for a few seconds, scanning the surroundings before launching himself straight up into the top of a huge nearby oak tree. He disappeared into the foliage and we never saw him again.

Before he left my hand he gave one final token of appreciation.

He crapped in my hand again!

Fred

(NOTE: Originally the story of Fred, like the story of Jack, was not to be included in this collection of memories and stories. But Grace pointed out there was a common theme between the 3 stories: a bird and a roadway. Plus it's really an entertaining tale. So if you're eager for this book to end, my apologies, but this won't take long to read. Or if you're enjoying my journey down memory lane then read slowly and drag the ending out.

It was '94 and we were driving from the Ramona Flea Market on the Westside of Jacksonville when I got a sudden glimpse of something that seemed impossible. I immediately pulled over onto the shoulder of the road and Grace asked what was wrong and I told her I thought I saw a cockatiel, sitting by the road. She gave me a strange look.

I left the car and as I walked back I did indeed see a beautiful male cockatiel calmly watching the cars pass within inches of him. I expected him to take flight as I approached but I stood over him and he calmly looked up at me. I extended my left arm outward and wiggled my fingers to distract him and when he looked at them I snatched him up with my right hand. He didn't struggle at all and when we got into the car, Grace wrapped him up in a towel and held him on her lap. Moments later I saw she had removed the towel and he was perched on her knee, enjoying the ride and making no attempt to escape. In fact he seemed to be quite comfortable and at ease. Once we were home I collected him and put him in a cage by the couch in the living room. He was a simply beautiful bird and immediately settled into his new surroundings. Obviously a lost pet, he loved to sit on my shoulder or lap and watch tv or simply join me as I read. If I didn't take him out of the cage he would sit as close to me as possible.

When he was taken out of the cage he never made an attempt to escape and soon the door to his cage was often left open and he enjoyed sitting on the top of it observing the events of the household.

I bought a book on Cockatiels with many full color photos and he loved to look at the pictures with me. He would sit on my shoulder and stare at the photos of the cockatiels with obvious interest. But if a picture was of a female cockatiel, he would squawk enthusiastically and dance along my shoulder in an obvious mating ritual. When I flipped the page he would slide down my arm, into my lap and try to flip the pages back!

He was obviously in love. Or at least lust.

What to do? Well the solution came from my sister Donna. Donna was in very bad health and knew she was dying. She also had Molly.

Molly was a female cockatiel and Donna begged me to take her and I did. Donna had owned Molly for many years and it was a huge relief to her to know her little bird was going to a good home. At first sight of her, Fred was so excited and he whistled enthusiastically at her. Probably a cockatiel version of a wolf whistle. He also would do a little dance and would sway back and forth. It reminded me of the nature shows on tv that showed the mating dances of various species of birds. Or it might have been an avian version of the movie DIRTY DANCING. Maybe he was trying to turn Molly on. So I put him in her cage.

She promptly kicked his ass.

She tore into him and feathers flew. I snatched him out to save his life. Molly was intent on preserving her virginity or possibly was a lesbian but she wanted nothing to do with him.

Or me.

She had never been handled or even out of her cage and when I approached her I got much the same treatment he did. I wanted to tame her down so she could leave her cage so I would don thick leather gloves and would hold her and stroke her while she tried to rip off my fingers through the gloves. And she was able to clamp down on my fingers even through the heavy leather. She was never able to inflict any actual pain but it wasn't due to lack of effort. Meanwhile Fred would be on my shoulder screaming advice and encouragement. Occasionally he would gather his courage and work his way close to her but she made her intentions towards him quite clear and he wisely did not get too close.

In a short time I was able to safely handle her and she accepted me so I decided to try and reunite her with Fred again. Once she realized he didn't have leather gloves she again tried to murder him.

If she had originally belonged to Lorena Bobbitt, instead of my sister, it might have gotten really ugly.

So for a period of time I put their cages side by side. He sat as close as possible to his True Love and she stayed as far away from The Rapist as the confines of her cage allowed.

Eventually an uneasy truce formed and I let Fred have conjugal visits but the peace never lasted long. She had a bad habit of snatching out the feathers on his head and before long he was totally bald. Telly Savalas bald. Not a good look on a cockatiel!

Plus his upper beak began to grow. And grow. Soon it was nearly 2 inches long and curved under his chin. Eventually Grace took him to the vet to have it trimmed. The vet took one look at this long beaked, totally bald cockatiel and burst out laughing.

It was quite a sight.

Well Molly was much older than Fred and she passed away after a few months, along with my sister. Fred was devastated and soon his heart broke and he was gone too. Wherever birds go after this life, I pray he found a loving mate.

But <u>not</u> Molly!

THANK YOUs

As always there are many people in the background who warrant mentioning. These are a few of them. My apologies to anybody I failed to thank.

MV Belyeu: Without MV's quick reaction of braking his car to avoid hitting Roscoe in the road, this would have been a 2 sentence book. Sadly MV died last year. He had a number of health issues and many years ago, he told me that he was unlikely to see his 30th birthday. Happily he lived into his late 60s. But a few years ago he was diagnosed with Stage 4 lung cancer. He was offered an experimental drug and it gave him another year. But he came over on a Sunday to visit us and I noticed he looked tired. Before leaving to go home, we hugged each other. It was the only time we did that but it felt like the right thing to do. Two days later I received the call. He had been found dead in his bedroom. Rest In Peace, Brother! We miss you.

Judy Carter: Judy's very generous gift of Roscoe's cage was a true blessing. It gave him a place to sleep, bathe, play and feel safe. He loved it and so did we!

Arianna DeFrank: Thanks for your friendship and sharing of your experience in raising a Cardinal and the wonderful stories and videos of Schnardz, the crippled Cardinal you rescued after his parents pushed him out of the nest. The poor bird had a clubfoot and could never survive on his own. But she successfully raised him and they are inseparable. The stories, pictures and videos you shared have brought me so much joy since I lost Roscoe.

Robert Chadwick and Lynn Thompson: Old friends and former co-workers, Robert designed the book cover and Lynn shared her publishing knowledge with me. Thanks to both of you.

Chad Kirkpatrick: My son has grown into a very fine man and I'm very proud of him. He laughs at the antics of his old man but I know, deep inside, he understands. But he has given me tremendous support in this project. First of all he bought me a new computer which works much better than the one I was struggling with and which made working on this book simpler. Then he has given me the technical support and knowledge I required to make this publishable. He calls his parents "cave people" because of our lack of all but the most simple bits of technical knowledge. He's right!

Volunteers: Thanks to the thousands of volunteers at bird rescues, wildlife centers and animal rehabilitation facilities. Your selfless dedication to our scaled, feathered and furry friends is wonderful. Just please answer the damn phone when people need your advice and help.

My Friends and Readers: So many friends, many unmet, gave me so much support by responding and sharing my FaceBook, Cardinal Cottage and other sites' posts and helped to spread the stories of The Crimson Prince. When you laughed at my jokes or sympathized with me in the moments of sadness you gave me such a warm feeling of companionship which meant a great deal to me. It was your encouragement that led to the development of this book.

I hope you are not disappointed. (There are no refunds...)

And most of all, I dedicate this book to THE ANGEL WHO WALKS ON THE EARTH, my wonderful wife Grace who nearly 50 years ago ignored BOTH of our mothers' advice to NOT marry me and so made me the luckiest and happiest man ever born. You have accepted my weird activities in trying to rescue the small and helpless and always lended a hand without (rarely) complaining. I love you!

A Final note (Finally)

In the event that Hollywood decides to make a blockbuster movie of this book, I have some suggestions for the cast: Playing me should be either Matt Damon or Tom Hanks. Playing Grace should be Jennifer Anniston or Scarlett Johansson.

And naturally the role of Roscoe would be played by Big Bird!

FACEBOOK

Here are just a few of my favorite Facebook posts. For those who followed him, they are a short trip down Memory Lane and then a few final photos:

FACEBOOK: LIFE WITH ROSCOE -Day 5

He's still alive!!

I have a great deal more respect for mama birds now. One baby bird is a lot of work. I can only imagine caring for a nest full. They have to find the food and bring it back, slam it down somebody's throat and then go back and do it again. We have a couple of Bluebird nesting boxes I put up and they raise 2-3 clutches each year. I buy mealworms that I put out for them but now I feel like I need to step up my efforts on their behalf.

Also there is a disgusting SNL (Saturday Night Live) skit I've seen a couple of times where the actors eat food and then "regurgitate" it into another actor's mouth, like a bird would do. I always feel like I'm doing it when I feed him.

Those worms taste like crap. LOL! And they don't help his breath at all...

FACEBOOK: LIFE WITH ROSCOE : Day 5 part III

Grace and I just fed His Majesty for (hopefully) the last time today. The sun has nearly set and all good birds should be settled in for the night.

Grace and I both had things to do today that could not include loud bossy birds so he had some alone time. Luckily we were able to stagger our time and he only had to go without food for two hours.

He acted like we were murdering him. When I got home I could hear him the complete length of the house. I rushed to the sunroom in order to stuff his gullet. The whole time I was feeding him he was giving me a good case of the stinky eye!

Apparently he was not amused.

But after he ate and had a good crap, he was in a better mood. So I decided to attack.

I got a shallow bowl of warm water, some Q tips and cotton balls. It was bath time. He was still coated in dried cat food from our original efforts to keep him alive. He was not at all attractive in that condition.

I placed him in the bowl of water and he did not appreciate the effort. Even the tiny rubber ducky did not amuse him. So he took flight and flew across the room before crashing with a THUMP onto the floor. A new record: almost 4 feet! I am still amazed that he seemed to enjoy being cleaner. Maybe he just didn't enjoy having his nether areas swimming in water.

Grace and I are still wondering what breed of bird he is. I again think mockingbird but unless he's a heckuva runt, he's going to have to grow out quite a bit before I can kick him out.

So he better get busy and learn to fly. REALLY fly, not these short aborted flights. But it's not totally his fault. His wings are still very short and while his feathers are coming in, he is still sadly lacking.

I retrieved him and he perched happily on my left forefinger as I took the cotton balls and Q tips and dipped them in the warm water and bathed him. Kind of an avian sponge bath. He didn't mind my efforts and actually seemed to enjoy them. And then, to confirm my fears, he flew in the opposite direction, all the way across the sunroom and landed on one of the fish carvings that hang on the walls. Totally horizontal flying and a nice landing too. He's getting the idea.

And so I had to climb up on a chair to retrieve him. Remember what I said about him landing in the wrong places? If I have to get a ladder to recapture him, it's definitely the wrong place.

Well as you can see, he has definitely made massive improvements in the feather department. He's covering up nicely but I'm curious as to why his neck is still bare. Chad claims he is really a vulture.

Maybe he's right.

Speaking of, I'm holding a contest to identify what type of bird he is. Or will be.

I'm starting to discount mockingbird as an option. Wrong color for a cardinal. Too heavy for a hummingbird. No longer resembles a Blue Jay.

I'm down to a California condor or a pterodactyl.

So tell me what you think Roscoe is. The winner gets a VERY lifelike replica of Roscoe. Complete with bird turd stained basket

FACEBOOK: LIFE WITH ROSCOE - Day 6

HOUSTON! WE HAVE A PROBLEM!

His Majesty was awake bright and early this morning and demanded his first meal of the day. I crammed his food down his little throat as required and stumbled back to bed.

Another day has started.

About an hour later, the appetizer had worn off and round two was called for. I pushed some more cat food into his maw when a mischievous look came into his eyes. I recognized the look but was too slow in reacting.

He launched himself from the handle of his basket and flew UP and over to the door sill. He had accomplished this feat the day before when I was not watching and it nearly gave me a minor heart attack. Not realizing he was able to fly upward I had frantically searched the room trying to find him. I was fearful one of our cats had slipped into the sunroom unnoticed and managed to get him. Before his short attempts at flying had only taken him vertically for short distances and then immediately downward. So this was a major step and a potential short term problem for us. He can now get to spaces and places we may not be able to retrieve him from. If he was ready to go free it wouldn't be a big deal. But he's still got a way to go.

FACEBOOK: LIFE WITH ROSCOE: Day 6 part II

Well it seems that Roscoe is likely a Cardinal which makes sense as there was a male Cardinal near the spot we found him. However that bird immediately vacated the area without making any effort to protect the young one and since Roscoe's coloring and features did not seem to be "Cardinal like", I did not consider the adult to be a prospect for "Father of the Year!", especially after he slipped away so swiftly. Often I wondered if the male was indeed Roscoe's blood kin and did I actually do him a favor by snatching him from the wild and giving him a life of luxury and safety.

And now it looks like he's ready to leave the nest. AGAIN!

I read some interesting information on baby Cardinals last night and according to it he is at the stage where they generally venture forth.

And most of them die.

They can "fly" at this stage but only in short bursts which he has proven numerous times. But they stay close at hand and their parents keep an eye on them. But he has to learn to eat without me cramming prepared food down his gullet and catering to his every need. So I am going to have to basically starve him into picking up his food and eating. Also I need to introduce him to fruits, bugs and seeds. Somehow I've got to teach him to crack sunflower seeds (and spit the shells).

Since I have no intention of setting him free until these violent rains we are having pass, it gives a few days. Plus I have to figure out where I can set him free and not have one of our cats lurking nearby.

(SIGH!) And I thought raising a teenage boy without killing him was tough.

Anybody have a Cardinal costume I can wear?

BIG disappointment.

Facebook: LIFE WITH ROSCOE: Day 6: part II

I fed the Feathered King only half of his normal rations this morning and put some in a bowl in his "suite" in the hopes he will learn to eat on his own. He must start this so I can release him soon

Then we left for 3 hours.

On the way back we bought 100 mealworms for him as "Live Food 101" is lesson #2. As Man does not live on bread alone, a wild bird will need to be able to hunt. Worms, crickets, grasshoppers should all be on the menu.

Upon returning we walked into the house to the sounds of birdie screams of pure agony. I doubt the Inquisition generated such sounds. The food in his bowl was untouched. He still expected to be fed, as any royalty would. Spoiled brat.

I gave him 2 morsels from the bowl to shut him up and then switched to the live worms.

First of all shoving a wriggling worm down a bird's throat is not an easy task. The worms don't seem to appreciate the gesture. Second, the recipient wasn't interested either. When we would finally get one in his gaping beak, he wouldn't swallow but kept it open while the hapless victim was struggling to escape.

Not an appealing sight.

We managed to send a couple of worms to their fate. For now he is quiet.

FACEBOOK: LIFE WITH ROSCOE - Day 7 Well it's been a week and he's just about fully feathered. Most probably a Cardinal because there's a tuft on the top of his head. Slight possibility it's a Tufted Titmouse but I severely doubt it.

He's still eating very well BUT not anything that will get him released. The cat food goes down easily but he's resisting the attempts to eat worms and insects. I fight to cram them down and he fights to avoid swallowing them. The worms are in a reverse form of Tug of War.

As soon as he is full he is eyeing the windows looking for a way to get outside. He can definitely fly although I have no idea how far. But when I see him lower his body I know it's in preparation of launching himself upward and I quickly move to block him. Sometimes I'm successful and sometimes I have to go retrieve him from wherever he lands.

Facebook: LIFE WITH ROSCOE Day 21

At sunrise I hear The Crimson Child wake up. He starts out with a few "Good morning world" chirps. Then the number and volume of his sounds increases. And increases. And increases.

The meaning of these new communications is quite obvious.

It's a demand for room service. From ME! His personal slave.

He's not at all discretely informing everybody that I am not meeting his strict morning requirements that begin with me getting up, dragging myself to him and opening the cage doors.

Once I do he will hop onto the door frame. Then launch himself into the air and he flies as fast as he can around the room 2 or 3 times. Then he returns to the top double doors (there are 3 sets) and watches me as I take small bungee cords and secure the top 2 sets of doors so they stay open.

Once he's sure I didn't screw this up he again flies at breakneck speed around the room some more.

This gives me time to prepare his breakfast, some plump wax worms. I keep them in a large plastic jar of sawdust.

Now I generally take the jar and sit in the recliner. I get comfy and then work the controls to lower the back and raise the legs. He lands on the left arm of the chair and enjoys a short ride while the chair reclines. I then pull out a worm and he hops over and takes it from my fingers and eats it. We repeat until he's full. Then he goes back into the cage or somewhere in the room.

Now all of this is done as quickly as possible to vainly attempt to avoid waking Grace.

I generally stay with him for a while. He will come back several times for additional worms and also to "clean" my beard of any dropped morsels of food or to clean out ear wax or go booger mining in the depths of my nostrils. The latter is not pleasant as he loves to pull HARD on my nostril hairs. It HURTS!

Well yesterday I committed a terrible sin. A CARDINAL SIN.

Instead of sitting in the recliner, I sat across the room on the couch. He went to the recliner arm as tradition dictates and waited for me to take my correct and approved position.

But I didn't move.

He could see me quite clearly but he also refused to move. First he called me then he started hopping up and down on the recliner arm. It was like a tiny red Rumpelstilskin stamping his feet in anger.

I didn't care. The sun was coming through the windows and would have blinded me in the recliner. I stayed put.

The slave was revolting. He didn't like it. He would not come to me.

And so some lucky wax worms were given a temporary reprieve and a barely longer life.

After my breakfast I returned and dutifully took my approved place and the world returned to normalcy.

FACEBOOK: Life With Roscoe Day 142

I think I've hit rock bottom.

I may need an intervention. Or to be Baker Acted.

Because it is chilly this morning, I brought His Majesty, The Emperor Of Easy Living, WARM WATER for his morning bath. WARM WATER!!! The Cardinals in the backyard are braving the weather as it is without the luxury of human slaves who cater to their every wish and whim.

On the plus side, he IS apparently enjoying it because he just hopped in and the water is flying everywhere.

Opps. Have to go. He just rang his bell for room service...

Facebook : Life WITHOUT Roscoe

This is going to be painful.

Yesterday I received a voicemail to call an investigator with the Wildlife Department for the State of Florida. I returned his call but did not reach him.

He called again today but missed me so I called him back. I wish I hadn't .

Seems somebody sent an "anonymous complaint" about us having Roscoe. I explained the whole story, especially about releasing him multiple times and him returning. I explained his living conditions and that he was happy, healthy and loved.

He listened but explained it was against the law to have a Cardinal as a pet and he was required to confiscate him and release him in a wildlife management area. There is a Federal Migratory Bird Law. I argued Cardinals are not migratory and he said they are included.

He said there were multiple complaints as the letter stated "We are a community of people upset at the treatment of this bird..."

Bullshit. There was only ONE complaint. I know because I was later supplied a copy of the letter. It was redacted to prevent me from identifying the author. ONE PERSON!

I have a fairly good idea of who might be responsible and they don't care about the bird but this is a strike against me personally. I am often guilty of speaking my mind and I know that sometimes my opinions are not well received.

I begged the officer to wait until Spring since it's cold and there is limited food available. He's giving me until Monday to turn him over.

As I'm typing this Roscoe is perched on my knee munching a wax worm. So damn cute.

I had always intended for him to be free. I never expected him to return to us or that I would become so attached to him.

This sucks.

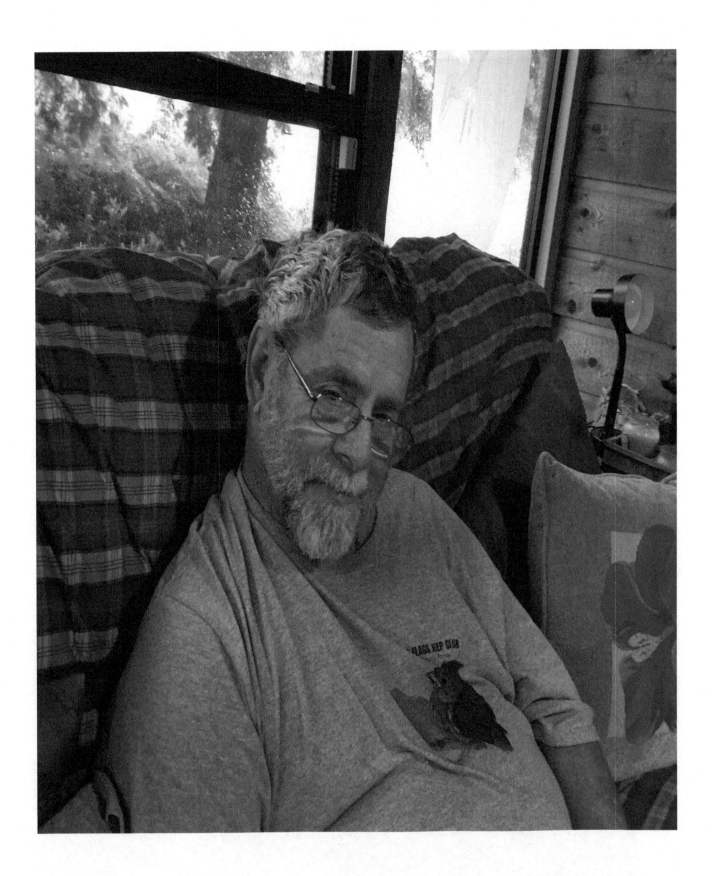

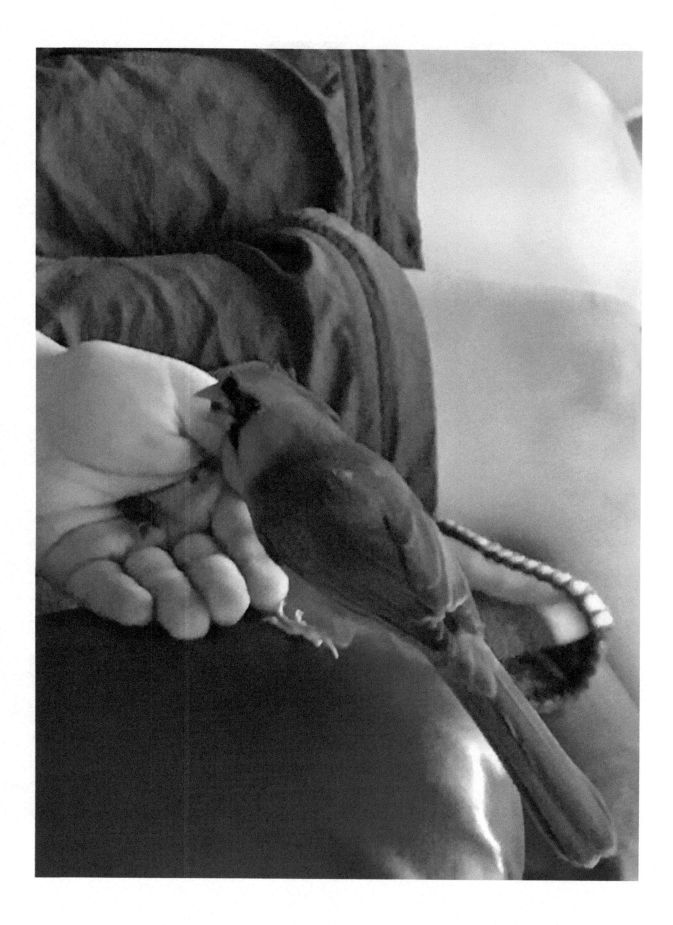

"Some birds are not meant to be caged, that's all. Their feathers are too bright, their songs too sweet and wild. So you let them go, or when you open the cage to feed them they somehow fly out past you. And the part of you that knows it was wrong to imprison them in the first place rejoices, but still, the place where you live is that much more drab and empty for their departure." *Stephen King*

Made in the USA
Columbia, SC
07 January 2022

53745031R00109